A Sea of Troubles

A SEA
OF TROUBLES
by J. J. McCoy

drawings by Richard Cuffari

A Clarion Book · THE SEABURY PRESS · *New York*

Grateful acknowledgment is made to the publisher
for permission to quote material from *So Excellent a
Fishe: A Natural History of Sea Turtles* by Archie Carr.
New York: Doubleday & Company, Inc., 1973.
Copyright © 1973 by Archie Carr. All rights reserved.

Library of Congress Cataloging in Publication Data

McCoy, Joseph J 1917–
    A sea of troubles.

    Bibliography.
    Includes index.
    SUMMARY: Examines the present-day threats to the
living and mineral resources of the world's oceans and the
political and economic conflicts involved in trying to
save the sea from irreversible damage.
    1. Marine ecology—Juvenile literature. 2. Marine
resources—Juvenile literature. [1. Marine pollution.
2. Marine resources conservation] I. Cuffari, Richard
1925–   ill. II. Title.
QH541.5.S3M23   333.9'5   74-22474
    ISBN 0-8164-3140-X

Contents

Author's Note · vii

1 · The Sea · 3

2 · The Fouling of the Sea · 8

3 · Danger in the Bays and Estuaries · 23

4 · Dominion over the Fish of the Sea · 40

5 · Plight of the Porpoises · 55

6 · Titans of the Sea · 69

7 · The Fur Seals · 85

8 · Sea Otters · 100

9 · Decline of the Sea Cows · 113

10 · Sea-going Turtles · 125

11 · Loners of the Arctic Ice Packs · 137

12 · Birds of the Sea and Shore · 151

13 · Return to the Sea · 165

Suggested Reading · 177

Index · 183

To Basia,

who lived with me near the sea and marvelled,
as I did, at its agelessness and durability.

Author's Note

A book about the troubles of the sea is more than a one-person task, for who can truthfully claim to know all there is to know about the vast ocean environment? Accordingly, I am indebted to many people, alive and dead, for help and guidance during the three years spent in research for this book.

The variety of contributors to the research is considerable, ranging from the ancient Greeks and their dolphin myths to Herman Melville and his epic sea novel, *Moby Dick*, on to Joseph Conrad's fascinating sea stories, and then to modern mariners, fishermen, ocean scientists, biologists, zoologists, ecologists, environmental protectionists, segments of industry, conservation organizations, and various government agencies.

I am especially grateful to the following persons and organizations for providing specific data on the problems of the sea:

Dr. John B. Pearce, Officer-in-Charge, Middle Atlantic Coastal Fisheries Center, Sandy Hook Laboratory, Highlands, New Jersey

Larry Ogren, diver-biologist, Sandy Hook Marine Laboratory

James Chess, marine biologist, Westinghouse Research Laboratories, La Jolla, California

James S. Young, marine biologist, Battelle N. W. Laboratories, Richland, Washington

Charles I. Gibson, marine biologist, Battelle N. W. Laboratories, Richland, Washington

Senator Ernest F. Hollings, Chairman, Subcommittee on Oceans and Atmosphere, Senate Commerce Committee

Fishery Division, Food and Agriculture Organization, the United Nations, Rome

Middle Atlantic Coastal Fisheries Center, Sandy Hook Marine Laboratory, Highlands, New Jersey

Office of Public Affairs, National Oceanic and Atmospheric Administration, Rockville, Maryland

National Science Foundation, Washington, D. C.

The National Wildlife Federation, Washington, D. C.

The Humane Society of the United States, Washington, D. C.

And a special note of thanks to my daughter, Lyza, for her help with the research and typing.

J. J. McCoy

A Sea of Troubles

· I ·

The Sea

Behold the sea: mysterious, moody, ever-changeable, a vast tract of water occupying seventy-one percent of the earth's surface. Often the sea is serene, but sometimes it becomes violent when lashed by strong winds. It displays a variety of colors: greens, blues, grays, with tints and tones in between. It has its own orchestra, a symphony of roarings, whisperings, boomings, lappings—now melodious and soothing, now discordant and frightening. And it is a huge repository of many forms of life, ranging from tiny plankton to gigantic whales.

People are both attracted and repelled by the sea, depending upon the circumstances under which they come into contact with it. Yet despite their awe and fear, human beings have been drawn to and utilized the sea and its tributaries, the bays and estuaries, for all of recorded history. Perhaps, aside from the obvious commercial reasons, this attraction to the sea is a natural response. At least it is if one accepts the prevailing scientific theory that all earth life began in the primeval sea many millions of years ago. It may be that man's tendency to embrace the sea, explore it, and dwell along its shores stems from some inner need to return to the sea-womb from which all life is said to have been delivered. It is not surprising, then, that the lure of the sea is not restricted to those persons who sail or live near it. Urbanite and suburbanite, mountaineer and plains-man are equally attracted to it, and some of the world's finest mariners come from regions that are far from the sea.

The sea represents many different things to these people, according to their life style, occupation, and interest. For some, it is a watery highway to distant lands and exotic ports. Fishermen regard the sea as a big cupboard from which they can help themselves to fish and shellfish. Industrialists and developers view the sea as a bonanza site for the exploitation of chemicals, minerals, and petroleum. Ocean scientists utilize the sea, surface and deeps, as an immense laboratory to further their knowledge about the ocean environment. Vacationists and pleasure-seekers consider the sea and its beaches as a world playground area. To the pilot and passengers of a jet transport, the sea is simply a region to cross to reach another continent. And small children know the sea as the source of shiny sand, spirally seashells, and scary waves.

Thus, for thousands of years the ocean environment has been a boon to humanity. It has carried the ships of many nations for trade, fisheries, and defense. It has served as a natural boundary for human territories. Out of the sea have come tremendous quantities of nutritious foods, raw petroleum, valuable minerals, precious metals, and useful chemicals. Great novels and works of art have been inspired by the various moods of the sea and the many events that have occurred in its waters.

Most important, the sea is a gigantic reservoir of energy. Its surface is never still, never completely at rest. There is always some degree of motion, even when it appears calm. When one reflects that approximately ninety-two percent of the earth's water is in the sea and that all of this water is subjected to constant change and movement, then it is not too difficult to understand why the sea serves as a source of energy.

The greatest exchange of energy takes place at the air-sea interface. The interface is the seemingly endless region where the atmosphere and sea appear to meet. At the air-sea interface, where the sun's energy penetrates into the sea, water heat and thermal currents are generated. The thermal currents flow downward as well as across the sea. Water vapor is absorbed into the atmosphere and later released in the form of rain. It is the sea that spawns hurricanes and typhoons. Winds beget waves and create currents that carry heat from the tropics to the polar regions. It is the wind sweeping and swirling over the sea that provides the main driving power for currents and waves. And it is the wind that supplies the initial force to set the sea in motion.

In return for its many bounties, though, man has not always been kind to the sea. His use of the ocean environment and its natural resources has often resulted in abuse. Too often the sea and its bays and estuaries are used as dumps and septic tanks for the disposal of all kinds of waste materials. Intense and sometimes violent fishery competition disrupts the serenity of the sea and has severely depleted stocks of fish, shellfish, and marine mammals in some regions. All in all, man's civilizations and technologies have placed a heavy burden on the sea, sometimes through ignorance, often deliberately.

The present troubles are global in distribution and origin. No single nation is responsible for the overburdening of the sea; many nations contribute to it. And no nation, not even those landlocked, is immune to the effects of the sea's troubles. Each nation, each person is dependent to some degree upon the sea for food, minerals, energy and recreation.

Thus, when a penguin thousands of miles from civilization ingests harmful amounts of DDT; when fish contain high levels of mercury; when shellfish in a bay or estuary are tainted with disease-bearing bacteria and viruses; when some nations encroach upon the territorial waters of others to take and deplete fish and shellfish stocks; when coastal zones, beaches, bays, and estuaries are cluttered with plastics, oil, pesticides, chemicals, metals, garbage, sewage sludge, and other refuse; when thousands of porpoises die in tuna nets, their bodies wasted; and when the natural and man-made laws of the sea are flouted or ignored—then all humanity, as part of the great web of life, becomes inexorably involved with the troubles of the sea.

What has happened to the ocean environment with its delicate ecosystems and their living resources—and what is still happening to them—stems mainly from our gross mismanagement of the sea. Of that there is no doubt, for the evidence of mismanagement and its results is becoming more visible each year.

To better understand the nature and extent of the damage caused by our mismanagement of the sea, we need to take a look at some specific examples of it. We need to know why and how they are caused, and by whom. And it is important that we know what can be done and what is or is not being done to correct or at least reduce the many abuses of the sea.

·2·

The Fouling of the Sea

Summer, 1972. The Atlantic Ocean off the coast of the United States. Three ships of the National Oceanic and Atmospheric Administration prowl the coastal waters. On board are various marine scientists. Their mission: conduct an ocean pollution survey from Cape Cod to the Caribbean Sea.

The scientists have no difficulty in locating pollution. It is all around them. A wide swath of floating oil, plastics, and tar stretches from Cape Cod to the Bahamas.

Although prepared to see considerable pollution, the scientists are astonished at the type and extent of the contamination. The waters off the eastern coast of the United States are indeed fouled beyond what most people expect.

Some pollutants occur in heavy concentration, often the size of a tennis ball. In certain coastal waters, the pollutants are so dense that they compress into spaghetti-like strips as they are sieved through the openings in the sample collection nets towed by the research ships.

The scientists are startled by these facts: marine pollution off the east coast covers fifty percent (about 80,000 square miles) of the area surveyed along the continental shelf; eighty percent (280,000 square miles) of the area in the Caribbean Sea to the Gulf of Mexico; and ninety percent (305,000 square miles) of the survey area north of the Antillean Island chain.

Extensive pollution is seen by the scientists off the eastern coast of the Bahamas. Here, the contamination stretches for three hundred miles, north to south, and for fifty miles, east to west. This region includes the Antilles current, a part of the Sargasso Sea—that immense section of the North Atlantic that lies midway between the Old and New Worlds.

To obtain a better idea of the extent of the pollution observed by the scientists, look at the map of the Atlantic Ocean containing the east coast of the United States, the Antilles, and the Caribbean and Sargasso Seas. The shaded portion represents the area of pollution they charted.

Ocean pollution is by no means confined to the east coast of the United States, or the west coast. Nor must it be thought that only western hemisphere waters are contaminated. Marine pollution is worldwide, whenever and wherever man's waste materials are dumped into the sea.

Pollution is not a recent phenomenon either. Since ancient times, people of nations bordering the sea or its

NORTH

ATLANTIC

Sargasso Sea

GULF OF
MEXICO

CARIBBEAN SEA

tributaries have cast their sewage and other wastes into the sea. Flotsam and jetsam, the wreckage of ships and their cargos found floating in the sea or washed up on shore, were, perhaps, the first visible pollution. But they posed no serious threat to the ocean environment. The sea was able to cope with them, for in time chemical actions, scavengers, the lashing of the winds and currents eventually reduced the flotsam and jetsam to relatively harmless matter.

As civilizations evolved and large cities appeared along the coasts of the continents, more and dangerous kinds of pollutants entered the sea. Cities, farms, and industrial plants dumped their waste products into bays, estuaries, and coastal waters. For centuries, the sea has been regarded as a bottomless waste receptacle with an unlimited ability to absorb and digest all kinds and amounts of waste materials.

This idea is erroneous, of course. True, the sea is capable of absorbing a great deal of waste, chemical and otherwise, without endangering the quality of sea water and natural resources. However, wastes dumped into the sea must be evenly distributed, not concentrated in certain areas. When wastes are distributed, the natural forces can break down the pollutants into harmless matter.

Unfortunately, heavy concentrations of pollutants occur in many sea areas throughout the world, mainly in the waters off the continents. These concentrations of pollutants are so heavy that the sea's natural forces cannot cope with them. A result is severe damage to the marine ecosystems, specific areas of the sea and their living and nonliving natural resources.

Actually, the sea already contains many of the chemicals and minerals now being poured into it from man's activities. It possesses nearly all of the known elements. Among them are oxygen, nitrogen, hydrogen, carbon, chlorine, sodium, calcium, magnesium, sulphur, boron, potassium, bromine, strontium, silicon, fluorine, argon, and phosphorous. In the sea are also found a number of metals, including copper, zinc, lead, mercury, molybdenum, gold, and nickel. Some areas of the seabed even contain diamonds.

But the sea's chemical and mineral components must be present in the proper concentrations. When they are not properly balanced, as in the case of continued dumping or flushing of chemicals and metals into bays and coastal waters, then the marine ecosystems are disrupted or upset.

It should be remembered that not all of the sea's pollution is caused by the direct or indirect dumping of wastes by man. A certain amount of natural pollution takes place. Matter is normally carried to the sea by rivers, glaciers, and winds. Millions of tons of silt, fine particles of soil suspended in water, contain chemicals and minerals. The silt is transported into the sea by rivers. Usually, heavy deposits of silt are found at the mouths of rivers or just beyond them in the sea. In time, however, currents carry pollutants away from the river mouths, far out to sea beyond the continental shelves and into the deeps.

The sea has managed to cope with the natural pollution over the centuries. But it is now experiencing great difficulty in handling natural pollution and the increasing amounts introduced by man's activities.

What are some of the more important pollutants caused by human beings? One common and increasing pollutant of the sea is oil. Most people who watch television or read newspapers are familiar with oilspills in bays and coastal waters. Oilspills are increasing. In the summer of 1974, twenty-four miles of beach along the North Shore of Long Island Sound in Suffolk County, New York, were closed to bathers because of a large oilspill. A 741-foot tanker was transferring oil to a barge when the spill took place. The oil, according to reports, was accidentally pumped into the waters of Long Island Sound instead of containers on the barge.

The majority of oilspills result from malfunctioning offshore oil wells, damaged tankers, or—as in the case of the Long Island spill—careless operations. But oilspills are not limited to these causes. Oil also leaks into the sea from refineries, automotive and industrial wastes, and other petroleum processing sources. It often reaches the sea through vaporization of petroleum products into the atmosphere. Later, the oil vapor is discharged into the sea at the air-sea interface.

It is not just the simple loss of oil that disturbs most conservationists and environmentalists. Oil floats on water, of course, and much of an oilspill can be recovered. What is of great concern is the harm that oil causes to the sea's living resources. Oil clots the feathers of seabirds, making it difficult for them to fly. Perhaps the greatest danger of oilspills to seabirds and waterfowl occurs when the birds ingest oil when trying to clean their plumage. When oil gets into the lungs of the birds, they die.

Oil from a spill often forms a cover over the surface of the sea. It excludes sunlight and interferes with the growth and development of plankton, the tiny animals and plants that are so vital to the marine food chains. An oilspill, then, does more than close down a beach to bathers. When uncontrolled, it can cause widespread damage—some of it irrevocable—to the particular eco-system in which it occurs.

Another source of pollution that has an impact on the ocean environment is the excessive amounts of nitrogen and phosphorus now being discharged into the bays and coastal waters. Nitrogen and phosphorus are elements necessary for life in the sea. Both are utilized by phytoplankton, the small plantlike organisms that grow in the sea and form the basis of the marine food chains. The two elements are used in photosynthesis, the process which helps to build carbohydrates in the green parts of the tiny marine plants.

Too much nitrogen and phosphorus, however, can result in an excessive growth of phytoplankton in a given area of the sea. If this heavy growth is not utilized by other members of the food chain, then an oxygen shortage may occur in the area. A low or depleted oxygen supply can seriously affect all of the living resources in a blighted ecosystem. In addition to their damaging effect on other marine life, the excessive growths of phytoplankton—often foul-smelling and unsightly—destroy the aesthetic qualities of a beach, bay, or coastal area.

Just how much or what concentration of nitrogen and phosphorus in a specific sea area is acceptable is not presently known. Available data are not complete enough to draw conclusions or even to make estimates. Many factors, including the rate at which excess nitrogen and phosphorus are diluted and the reaction of sea creatures in the area, are involved in the sea's ability to handle excessive amounts of these two elements. For example, if the increased plant growth produced by excessive nitrogen and phosphorus is consumed by members of a particular food chain (for example, fish and sea turtles), then there is no problem. Instead, there would probably be an increased yield in fish and other marine life. This process is known as *enrichment* and, when controlled, might be considered a beneficial effect of pollution.

Most bays and coastal waters of developed nations now contain excessive nutrients. This is especially true of those regions where raw sewage is flushed into the sea. The dumping of sewage into bays and coastal waters is a relatively cheap and easy way to get rid of it. That is why it is being done today. In the long run, however, this method of sewage disposal is not only harmful to sea life but a waste of valuable nutrients. Sewage can be treated to reclaim nitrogen and phosphorus. Experiments have shown that treated sewage (that is, sewage in which harmful bacteria have been killed) is an excellent fertilizer for agricultural use. Yet many cities and towns continue to dump their sewage into the sea.

Paper pulp solids and liquids are another source of pollution in the sea. Effluents from paper manufacturing plants are discharged into rivers, bays, and coastal waters. They cause considerable pollution in Puget Sound; the Atlantic coastal waters off Georgia, South Carolina, and Maine; the Canadian maritime provinces; Sweden; and the Soviet Union. This type of pollution is especially harmful to the fish and shellfish industries of these regions.

When suspensions of paper pulp solids are dumped into a river or bay, they increase the turbidity of the water. What happens is that the water becomes cloudy or opaque, excluding sunlight that is vital to the process of photosynthesis. In waters choked with paper pulp effluents, this vital process is stopped. The result is often lifeless waters.

Wood chips and fibers separate from other paper pulp material and sink to the bottom of a river, bay, or estuary. Here, they form a layer that smothers benthic or bottom-dwelling fish and other marine life. Bacteria consume the oxygen in the sea bottom sediments, releasing methane and ethylane gases, which are toxic to living organisms. The liquid part of paper pulp effluents also demands oxygen and, together with the solids, soon uses up the oxygen supply in the water.

Ironically, the technology necessary to clean up paper pulp pollution is available. Some paper mills, because of public protest and pressure, have already taken steps to reduce pollution. For instance, some paper mills may use less water. They also recycle and recover a large portion of the effluents. Unfortunately for the sea, many paper mills have yet to begin a cleanup or reduction in their pollution.

We do not often think of metals as pollutants, yet certain metals are now polluting the ocean environment at an alarming rate. One such metal is mercury. Questionable as well as toxic levels of mercury have been found in fish used for human consumption.

Less than a decade ago, a number of people living in the Japanese fishing village of Minimata were afflicted with what became known as Minimata disease. This disease caused death, brain damage, paralysis, loss of speech, hearing, and sight. It also attacked fetuses in the womb, and many children born to parents affected by the disease were usually deformed or otherwise damaged for life. Some children were born retarded, blind, and deaf.

What caused Minimata disease? Scientists discovered that it was caused by mercury in the fish eaten by the people. The source of the mercury was traced to waste material dumped into coastal waters by a chemical company in the village. Fish became contaminated with the mercury, and when the villagers ate the fish, they were poisoned in turn. The chemical company was forced to stop dumping its mercury waste in the coastal waters after nearly ten thousand people had been poisoned.

Industry alone is not responsible for the rising mercury levels in the sea. Changes in the landscapes and landforms of the continents are a source of mercury pollution. Agricultural, mining, and construction activities disturb and dislodge the earth's surface solids, such as soil and rock. These disturbances allow more mercury vapor and gaseous mercury to escape into the atmosphere. Eventually, the mercury vapor and gas are transported to the sea, with the exchange taking place at the air-sea interface.

Lead is another metal now reaching the sea in increased amounts. The long-range effects of increased lead in the ocean environment is not presently known. Nevertheless, the absence of such data is no excuse for the continuous overloading of the sea with this potentially dangerous metal. We do know that lead is toxic to birds and mammals. And hospitals all over the United States have admitted small children suffering from lead poisoning after having eaten chips of paint containing this toxic metal.

Emissions from internal combustion machines, primarily automobiles and trucks, are the main source of lead pollution. Lead is used in gasoline as an anti-knock additive. Most of the lead burned in the internal combustion machines eventually reaches the sea. Also, an increase in world smelting operations (the refining or extraction of metals from ore) has raised the levels of this metal in various snowfields and in the sea.

Added to the metals being dumped into the sea are many chemicals, including pesticides used in agriculture and public health activities. Some of the pesticides, particularly DDT, aldrin, dieldrin, and BHC (Ben-zyl-hexa-chlor-ide) are hazardous to marine and human life. They are usually present in the atmosphere in the form of gases or are found on particles of matter, such as dust and soil.

In 1974, the United States Environmental Protection Agency ordered the manufacturer of aldrin and dieldrin to stop producing these highly toxic chemicals. Both aldrin and dieldrin accumulate in the fatty tissues of the animal body when taken in through the food chain and are suspected cancer-causing agents.

More than ninety percent of these two pesticides is applied to soil in cornfields. Erosion, caused by wind and water runoff, carries the pesticides into creeks and rivers and eventually into the sea. Even the halting of production of these two pesticides will not immediately reduce the threat, for the sea already contains unknown amounts or levels of the chemicals.

Though the long range effects are not fully known, these and other pesticides pose a most serious threat to human and marine life. A variety of pesticides are found in seafood and other food. These include chemicals that cause cancer (carcinogens), mutations (mutagens), and malformities (teratogens).

Another highly toxic chemical now entering the sea is known as PCB (Poly-chlor-in-ated-bi-phe-nyl). About twenty-five percent of the world production of PCB eventually leaks into the environment. Of this twenty-five percent, twenty enters the atmosphere and is ultimately carried into the sea by global winds. The remaining five percent goes into rivers and eventually finds its way into the waters of the continental shelves.

PCB is toxic to animal life. Concentrations of 100 parts per million have been found in fresh and coastal waters of Japan. A number of persons have died as a result of eating rice oil contaminated with PCB. Yet this dangerous chemical is still flushed into rivers and coastal waters.

Freons, colorless gases used in refrigeration and aerosol cans, also join the man-made chemical stew in the ocean environment. Some freons are manufactured at the rate of more than a half-million tons a year on a world basis. Nearly all of this amount is released into the atmosphere (every time an aerosol can or bomb is used, some freon escapes into the atmosphere) and is transported to the sea.

The sea must also contend with bacteria and viruses carried in raw sewage and other solid wastes. Various bacteria capable of causing animal and human diseases have been isolated from bays and coastal waters. A few years ago, sixty cases of cholera in human beings appeared in Naples, Italy. This cholera outbreak resulted from the victims' having eaten polluted mussels taken from the Bay of Naples.

Bacterial pollution of bay and coastal waters of the United States is increasing each year. As a result of bacterial pollution, health authorities have been forced to close a number of beaches to bathers in New Jersey. Also, health authorities in Nassau County, New York, recently warned people about swimming in the Ouimet Canal in

Mineola, Long Island. The canal water was polluted with bacteria that caused intestinal disorders.

In samples taken from the canal, the bacteria count was greater than 240,000 per 100 milliliters of water. Since there is an interchange of tidal water from Long Island Sound and the Ouimet Canal, it is believed the bacteria were carried into the canal from the sea.

The overburdened sea is further contaminated by way of nuclear testing. Nuclear weapon testing by the United States, the Soviet Union, and other nuclear powers is the primary cause of artificial radionuclides found in the sea.

The present concentration of artificially-produced radionuclides, according to the Food and Agriculture Organization of the United Nations, is 109 curies. In simple terms, a curie is that amount of radioactive substance undergoing decay or decomposition at so many disintegrations per second. It is used to measure the level of radioactivity.

Most of the radioactive pollutants remain on the surface of the sea. They are found mainly in the northern hemisphere, since most nuclear testing is done in that portion of the world. Tritium, an isotope (an isotope is one, two, or more elements that have the same atomic number and the same chemical behavior, but are different in atomic weight and properties) of hydrogen, also enters the sea by way of nuclear reactor operations and fuel processing.

The sea must also endure thermal pollution from the warm water discharged from nuclear and other power plants. Thermal pollution is harmful to marine animals and plants. Certain species of fish are highly susceptible to radical changes in water temperature, and when they enter warm water from power plants, they go into shock and die.

These are the major pollution troubles of the sea. Yet, despite the fact that the ocean environment is indeed polluted far beyond the expectations of scientists and environmentalists, there are still many questions that haven't been answered. For instance, what amounts of specific pollutants are now entering the sea? How do these pollutants get into the sea? How are they transported from their original point of entry; that is, are they carried by winds, circulation of currents, upwelling of sea water, or by other means? Do marine organisms manage to break down pollutants? What are the final resting places, if any, of the various pollutants in the sea? Finally, and most important, what effects do these pollutants have on marine life and on man himself? The marine scientists aboard the three ships of the National Oceanic and Atmospheric Administration were seeking the answers to these and other questions involving pollution of the sea. What the scientists aboard the research vessels plying the Atlantic coastal waters observed was but a fraction of the fouling of the sea. It was, to use a familiar phrase, just the tip of the iceberg. The true extent of marine pollution may never be ascertained in this century. But one fact is certain: everything has its saturation point and the sea is no exception. Sooner or later, if the fouling of the sea is not reduced, many oceanic regions will become true dead seas.

·3·

Danger in the Bays
and Estuaries

The Atlantic Ocean, two miles offshore of Bayhead, New Jersey. A scuba diver swims down toward a wrecked ship. It is the *Delaware* and it lies in seventy feet of water.

Now the diver is just above the wreck. Several fish swim sluggishly out of openings in the ship's hull. They are ocean pout *(Macrozoarces americanus)*, bottom-dwelling fish. The diver notices that the fish are in distress. Their gill movements are greatly exaggerated. Some of the pout are bloated beyond their normal size. And their skins are faded in color.

More fish are seen by the diver as he swims around the wreck. They are cunners *(Tautogolabrus adspersus)*, relatives of the spiny-fin wrasse fish found in waters near the British isles. The cunners are also in difficulty: some are squeezed into crevices in the ship, mouths agape, fins erect. Others swim about in a confused manner.

Next, the diver propels himself over to where some lobsters lie outside their holes. The lobsters make no attempt to scurry away as the diver approaches them. They remain still. The diver picks up a lobster and examines it. He notes that the claws are loose and extended. Upon closer inspection, the diver sees that the lobsters are dying.

Elsewhere around the wrecked *Delaware*, the diver observes dead rock crabs and dying mussels. He takes a last look around the murky waters near the wreck. Then, planting both feet on the sea bottom, he pushes off for the swim to the surface.

What did it all mean? What had caused the drastic behavioral and physical changes in the pout and cunner fish? And what was killing the lobsters, rock crabs, and mussels?

In an effort to find the answers, two biologists from the Middle Atlantic Coastal Fisheries Center's Sandy Hook Marine Laboratory, Larry Ogren and James Chess, made dives to the wrecked *Delaware*. They also visited other shipwrecks in New Jersey coastal waters. Many dead and dying fish and shellfish were seen by the biologists in coastal waters extending along the New Jersey coast from Seabright southward to Surf City, a distance of about forty-five miles. Most of the dead and

dying lobsters, crabs, mussels, clams, and fish were found on or near shipwrecks.

The biologists noted that the trouble spots or kill areas were limited to shipwrecks lying in eighty-five feet of water or less. At one wreck site, a ship once known as the *Mohawk*, the divers noticed very little marine life.

After making repeated dives, the biologists evaluated the situation. First, they found no great variation in the water temperature. It was more or less normal for that time of year—fall. Second, low dissolved oxygen levels were noted in samples of water taken from the site of the *Delaware*. Water samples from other shipwreck sites also showed a decrease in oxygen. Visibility in the water ranged from near zero to twenty meters during the dives.

Was it the low oxygen level that killed the marine life near the shipwrecks? It was a possibility. It was not ruled out by the biologists, although they knew there might be other reasons for this marine kill. For example, the so-called red tide that appears from time to time in New Jersey coastal waters might have been the cause. When high levels of nutrients are introduced into bays and coastal waters, and when the sun and sea temperature are favorable (usually in summer), then excessive blooms of algae and plankton, known as red tide, may be expected. In 1972, a red tide caused an outbreak of shellfish poisoning in New England coastal waters. But while red tides often kill or paralyze clams, oysters, and mussels, they do not affect crabs.

Thus, an important consideration in the fish and shellfish kills near the shipwrecks was pollution. New

Jersey coastal waters received tons and tons of domestic and industrial wastes from nearby cities. The decomposition of organic matter in the wastes could have produced the low oxygen levels in the waters around the wrecks. One clue that supported this theory was that dead crabs and lobsters found in the waters off Point Pleasant, New Jersey, had their gills clogged with waste material.

This kind of kill is not limited to Atlantic coastal waters; other coastal waters around the world have similar problems. What is most alarming about such pollution is that the world's bays, estuaries, and coastal waters are the lifelines of the sea. They are the habitat of most living marine resources. The coastal waters over the continental shelves are especially rich in marine life.

The continental shelves are the undersea land areas that slope gradually away from the edges of the continents toward the deeps. Oceanographers have set an arbitrary limit on the depth of the water at the end of the continental shelf: If there is no shallow break in the slope of the shelf, then the sea end of the shelf is considered to cease at a depth of about 1,800 feet. Beyond the continental shelves are other undersea land areas, such as the continental slope, rise, Abyssal Plain, and finally, the ocean bottom or deep.

Dense populations of fish are found in the waters over the continental shelves. The great fishing sites of the world, with few exceptions, are in the relatively shallow waters over the continental shelves. But because of their proximity to the continents, these waters are exposed to pollution.

Bays and estuaries (An estuary is that water area where the sea meets the mouth of a river. It includes tidal marshes.) are also fertile regions for marine life, especially fish, shellfish, and waterfowl. Even fish that dwell in the deeper waters of the sea for most of their lives return to bays and estuaries to feed and spawn. Yet these vital marine resource regions are being polluted at an alarming rate each year.

Such high levels of pollution threaten the entire food chain in the bays and estuaries, starting with the bottom link of the food chain, the plankton. Most organic matter in the sea is in the form of plankton. Plankton is divided into *Phytoplankton,* very small floating plantlike organisms, and *zooplankton,* feeble swimming or floating animals. Directly or indirectly, all marine life is dependent upon plankton.

Phytoplankton need sunlight and sea chemicals for growth. The sun pierces the sea to a depth of perhaps five hundred feet or less in most bays and estuaries. The area where the sun penetrates the sea is known as the *euphotic zone.* It is in this region that photosynthesis—the formation of carbohydrates by the action of the sun on the chlorophyll of the tiny marine plants—takes place.

Photosynthesis changes sea chemicals into a primary food that is consumed by zooplankton and by some larger marine animals. Chemical nutrients are naturally replaced in the sea by the excreta from sea animals and bacterial action in the decomposition of dead fish, mammals, and plants.

In turn the abundance of marine life is related to the

availability of phytoplankton and zooplankton. In shallow water areas chemical nutrients are stirred up by the motion of the water. They are transported to the euphotic zones where they support the growth and development of fish and other marine creatures. The Grand Banks off the Newfoundland coast are an excellent example of a fertile euphotic zone. Consequently, the Grand Banks fishing region attracts fishermen from all sea-going nations because of the abundance of fish.

Pollution, naturally, interferes with or destroys these vital life actions in the bays, estuaries, and waters over the continental shelves. When favorable conditions prevail, that is, when there is sufficient sunlight and sea chemicals, phytoplankton may multiply by as much as three hundred percent in one day. But their growth is sharply curtailed or completely stopped by landfill, dredge materials, industrial waste, and other pollutants.

While chemicals and pesticides are dangerous to fish and shellfish, there is the additional problem of thermal pollution. Unregulated flows of hot water effluents into bays and coastal waters are a primary cause of mass fish kills. A few years ago, thousands of migrating young menhaden *(Brevoortia tyrannus),* an important commercial fish, were killed by thermal pollution in Long Island Sound.

Scientists want to learn more about the overall effects of thermal pollution on fish and other marine life. But it is known that hot water effluents can be lethal to fish. Marine biologists James S. Young and Charles I. Gibson studied schools of young menhaden swimming from cold water into areas warmed by the discharges from power plants.

Young menhaden usually migrate along the shores and parallel to them about one kilometer (five-eighths of a mile) offshore. They swim in rather tight formations or schools. During a scuba dive, the two biologists noticed that when the menhaden entered the warm water, they immediately went into a thermal shock. After struggling and gasping near the surface for a minute or two, the young fish then sank to the bottom of the Sound. Some of the stricken fish attempted to swim upward, but when they again came into contact with the warm water, they finally sank back to the bottom where they eventually died.

The sinking to the bottom was a variation of fish kills caused by chemicals and pesticides. For example, fish poisoned by endrin, aldrin, and other chlorinated hydrocarbon compounds in rivers and lakes remain and die on the surface. Therefore, the extent of such a kill is readily visible.

This was not the case with the menhaden killed by thermal pollution. They sank to the bottom, and an actual death count or estimate was difficult. Biologists Young and Gibson also found that many of the dead menhaden on the bottom of Long Island Sound were eventually transported by currents into deeper waters of the sea. Here, they were disposed of by benthic scavengers, crabs and other sea animals, that live near or on the sea floor. Nevertheless, the biologists estimated that the total kill of menhaden by thermal pollution may have been as much as one hundred thousand fish.

One important source of this thermal pollution is electrical generating plants. In the Long Island Sound region (which includes parts of New York, Connecticut, and the northeastern tip of New Jersey), the concentrated human population demands a vast amount of electrical energy. There are at least twenty plants that return warm water into the Sound and its tributaries. Further, the United States Environmental Protection Agency estimates that a tremendous amount of warm water will continue to be flushed into Long Island Sound during the next two decades. When this occurs, more and larger fish kills can be expected.

Thermal pollution is not the only hazard posed by the power plants along or near bays and coastal waters. Nuclear power plants in particular cause other serious ecological problems for the marine environment. New Jersey's Department of Environmental Protection reported that the nuclear generating station located ten miles south of Toms River contributed to major disturbances in the marine ecosystems of the region.

For instance, the water intake screens used by the station annually trap more than thirty thousand blue crabs and twenty thousand winter flounder. Also, approximately 150 tons of zooplankton, 100 million fish larvae, and 150 million fish eggs are lost each year when they pass through the condensers used by the power station.

Nuclear and regular power stations also cause changes in the type of water in estuaries. Ordinarily, estuarine waters are brackish; that is, they contain a mixture of fresh and salt water. Some power stations return too much water with a high salt content, thus creating an imbalance in the fresh and salt water levels. Such a change destroys spawning and nursery areas used by a variety of marine organisms.

Added to the chemicals, hot water, and metals now being flushed into the sea are huge quantities of solid wastes such as dredge materials and sewage sludge. Dredge material is the scoopings or scrapings from the bottom of rivers and other waterways. Sewage sludge is the slimy, oozy deposit or sediment from sewage tanks or processing plants. Both dredge material and sewage sludge are high in organic content.

These two types of waste pose special problems. They do not readily dissolve and therefore do not integrate with the biological systems in the area. Also, since they contain little in the way of inorganic solids, they do not mix or blend with the lower waters of a bay or estuary. Finally, these organic wastes can be transported long distances from their original point of entry.

Solid wastes, according to Dr. John B. Pearce, Officer-in-Charge of the Sandy Hook Marine Laboratory, may be harmful to benthic life communities. Often the solid wastes kill marine organisms by simply burying them or by decreasing the oxygen levels through bacterial reduction.

The injurious effects of solid wastes are not limited to the waters of bays and estuaries. Wastes dumped farther out in the sea can also prove harmful to marine life. In a research project, a number of bales of pressed domestic refuse (that is, waste from nonindustrial sources, such as homes) was dumped in two hundred meters of water off the coast of the British Virgin Islands. After being submerged for three months, the bales were hauled on board the research ship, *RV Advance.*

Scientists aboard the ship, according to Dr. Pearce, removed various materials from the bales for laboratory analysis. A most significant finding was the presence of coliform bacteria. These bacteria are characterized, when viewed under a microscope, by small holes, which cause them to resemble tiny sieves. Coliform bacteria are usually found in animal intestinal tracts and in dirty water and are capable of causing severe intestinal disturbances in human beings.

When the bales of refuse were first placed on the deck of the *Advance,* the scientists noticed a strong odor of hydrogen sulphide—a smell similar to that of rotten eggs. There were some black stains on the bales. Later, as the bales became more exposed to air, the stains turned gray in color. What all of this meant to the scientists was that a colony of oxygen-reducing bacteria was present on the bales and therefore at the site where the bales had rested in the sea.

The scientists were impressed by the fact that the bales had decomposed at a slow rate after being submerged for three months. But they were more impressed with the discovery of the coliform bacteria. Why? Scientists have long believed that sea water acts as a bactericide that kills or weakens coliform bacteria. But the active colonies of coliform bacteria on the bales brought up from the bottom of the sea seemed to refute this theory.

Since this project demonstrated that coliform bacteria can exist and even thrive in deep sea water, those industries and municipalities dumping solid wastes should be warned that such a practice may well provide a medium for the growth of bacteria harmful to human and marine life.

In Dr. Pearce's opinion, future studies of refuse placed in the sea should include an examination of the quality or condition of the waste materials in submerged bales. This is particularly important for refuse dumped into shallow waters of bays and estuaries. The limited decay of the bales submerged off the British Virgin Islands points up the need for waste quality studies. Consider these findings: newspapers in the bales were still readable after three months in sea water, almost all of the cloth materials were intact, and cotton and wool yarns showed no signs of decomposition, even when examined under a microscope. Although no hard or fast conclusions can be drawn from this one research project, it should be apparent that we cannot always expect rapid decay of refuse even when dumped in the deep sea.

Among all the kinds of solid wastes now being dumped in the sea, garbage and sewage sludge are perhaps the most controversial. Many coastal cities and municipalities claim they must dump these wastes in the sea. Their reason is simple: They are running out of land areas for dumps. The Hackensack Meadowlands Commission in northeastern New Jersey stated recently that its area dumps and landfills will be full in two years. In addition to the scarcity of land for dumps is the fact that air pollution controls now prohibit the burning of wastes in many communities.

Yet the refuse must go somewhere. Otherwise—as some city officials maintain—cities and towns will be buried under mountains of garbage, sewage, sludge, and trash. Many persons, particularly those charged with the responsibility of getting rid of wastes, think the bays, estuaries, and coastal waters are the most practical places in which to dump the ever-increasing loads of refuse.

Disposal of sewage sludge is an especially thorny issue. Sewage is mass-produced in cities and towns. Most cities and towns along coastal waters have been dumping sewage sludge into the bays and estuaries for years. When informed that they must obtain a permit to dump sludge into the sea, the various officials handling the sewage disposal problem become irate. They state that if they cannot use these areas as dumping grounds for sewage sludge, all sorts of serious problems will arise. They point out that sewage is accumulated each day. And, as one Philadelphia official stated, "You can't tell people to stop going to the bathroom."

Money is a prime factor in the disposal of sewage sludge. The City of Philadelphia must now haul sewage sludge fifty miles out to sea, instead of dumping it in Delaware Bay. The cost to taxpayers is about fifty dollars a ton. If Philadelphia has to haul the sludge one hundred miles out to sea, another fifty dollars a ton will be added to the sewage disposal bill.

When compared with other sewage sludge disposal methods, ocean dumping is probably the cheapest way to get rid of the sewage. Spreading the sludge on the land, as Chicago must do at the present time, costs about seventy dollars a ton. Drying and burning the sludge, even if air pollution laws were relaxed or repealed for this purpose, would cost taxpayers eighty dollars a ton, plus millions for equipment.

There is conflicting scientific testimony on the dangers of sewage sludge to the ocean environment. A study conducted by scientists at the Franklin Institute Research Laboratories and Jefferson University in Philadelphia failed to show that the dumping of sewage sludge in the sea caused any harm to the marine environment. Dr. Robert A. Earb of the Franklin Institute thought that ocean dumping was an "environmentally superior method" of disposal.

But in the summer of 1974, another marine scientist, Dr. William H. Harris of Brooklyn College, had a different opinion on the hazards of sewage sludge. Dr. Harris studied the effects of dumping sewage in 240 locations off Long Island's South Shore. He discovered pockets of sewage sludge a quarter of a mile off Atlantic Beach, an area used by many people for bathing.

These pockets of slimy sewage sludge appear to be moving closer to the actual swimming section of Atlantic Beach, according to Dr. Harris. He believes that the swimming waters will be contaminated by disease-bearing sewage sludge by the summer of 1976. Sewage sludge is a potential carrier of microorganisms causing hepatitis and encephalitis. Added to this hazard are heavy metals that somehow get into the sludge and enter the food chain by way of clams and fish. Some of the metals can cause serious illness or other ailments in human beings.

But two federal agencies, the National Oceanic and Atmospheric Administration and the United States Environmental Protection Agency disagree with Dr. Harris' findings and conclusions. Spokesmen for these two agencies stated that the sewage sludge creeping toward Long Island beaches presented no threat to swimmers. Their statements were based on an inspection of eight locations containing sewage sludge—as opposed to 240 sites examined by Dr. Harris. The two agencies did agree, though, that it will be necessary to find new sewage disposal areas farther offshore in the near future.

Ocean dumping is now regulated under the authority of the Marine Protection, Research, and Sanctuaries Act of 1972. The Act bans the dumping of high-level radioactive wastes, chemicals, and biological warfare agents in the sea. Other wastes (except dredge materials) may be dumped only with a permit and subject to certain regulations established by the Federal Environmental Protection Agency. Since dredging is performed by or under the supervision of the Army Corps of Engineers, the dumping of dredge materials is considered an Army problem. The patrolling or surveillance of ocean dumping is the responsibility of the United States Coast Guard. Research and the establishment of marine sanctuaries (for example, sea areas where no dumping is allowed) are the province of the National Oceanographic and Atmospheric Administration, United States Department of Commerce.

However, since the provisions of the Marine Protection, Research, and Sanctuaries Act became effective in 1973, ocean dumping has increased. Some of the permits being issued are not in the best interest of the particular marine environment that is involved in the dumping. Also, there is a strong feeling among a number of environmentalists that the ocean-dumping control program is not functioning as well as expected. One reason is a lack of funds. Another is a shortage of manpower. More important, it seems that the technology necessary to control or reduce ocean-dumping problems is, for some unknown reason, inadequate. It lags far behind pollution control technology on the land.

There is evidence to show that our ocean-dumping policies and programs need to be reevaluated. The criteria of the Federal Environmental Protection Agency are actually weaker than those established by the International Convention on the Prevention of Marine Pollution by dumping of wastes and other matters. Thus, we are in the position of telling other nations that we subscribe to stringent controls on ocean dumping but not in American waters.

Despite conventions, laws, and treaties, ocean dumping continues. Scientists contradict one another as to the extent of marine pollution and the danger it poses to our bays, estuaries, and coastal waters. City officials insist they must dump their refuse and sewage sludge into the sea because it is the cheapest way to get rid of it. Industry seeks permits to dump chemicals and other harmful wastes into the bays and estuaries. Unscrupulous persons and organizations flout ocean-dumping regulations and discharge their wastes into the sea at night, dodging the shorthanded Coast Guard patrols.

While individual scientists and government agencies haggle over the pros and cons of ocean dumping, the sea continues to receive increasing loads of waste materials. It is seen by scuba divers who probe deeper into the watery problem than some scientists and environmental protection agencies. These divers find dead and dying fish and shellfish. They push through dense growths of phytoplankton and algae caused by the discharge of excessive nutrients into the bays and estuaries. For them and other persons who have seen the extent and effect of marine pollution, the danger in our bays and estuaries is very real.

·4·

Dominion over the Fish of the Sea

The sea has provided man with food fish for thousands of years. In the beginning, there was enough for all. No people, no nation went without fish, for the great ocean environment seemed to have an unlimited supply. Then, as human populations increased there came a demand for more and more fish. Some nations developed aggressive and efficient fishery industries and took greater quantities of fish from the sea than others. Soon the stocks of important food fish dwindled to alarmingly low numbers. And as the stocks decreased, fishing nations entered into intense and sometimes violent competition for the declining supply of fish.

The North Atlantic off the coast of Iceland. Forty British fishing boats trawl for cod within fifty miles of the Icelandic coast. Far to the east, two British frigates prowl the sea, ready to lend a hand to the trawlers if the need arises.

The British trawlers have been warned that Iceland has extended her territorial waters from the old twelve-mile limit to a new limit of fifty miles. But the British fishermen stubbornly hold to the old limit.

Icelandic patrol boats move in and out among the trawlers. Some fishing lines are cut by patrol boat crews. There is tension on both sides. A few fishermen glance anxiously to the east, hoping to see their backup force of frigates steaming toward them. But the frigates do not appear. The sea is dotted only by the trawlers and Icelandic patrol boats.

Still, the British trawlers do not yield to the Icelandic boats. They plod through the rough waters, hauling in codfish. Off by herself is the 884-ton trawler, *Everton*, out of the British port of Grimsby.

Now the Icelandic Coast Guard ship, the *Aegir*, steams toward the *Everton*. The *Aegir*'s captain hails the *Everton* and motions for her to sail out beyond the fifty-mile limit. The *Everton* ignores the request and continues to trawl for cod.

Again, the *Aegir* warns the *Everton* to stop fishing in Icelandic territorial waters. And again, the *Everton* refuses to obey.

Suddenly, two warning shots are fired from the guns of the *Aegir*. The shots are blanks. But the *Everton* ignores them and continues to trawl. Now the *Aegir* closes in on the *Everton*. This time the *Aegir*'s guns open fire with live ammunition. Several shells hit the *Everton*, but she is not disabled. Her captain orders more speed, and the *Everton* moves away from the *Aegir*.

There is a short chase. But the *Everton* pulls away from the *Aegir*. Only when the *Everton* is beyond the territorial limit does the *Aegir* abandon the pursuit and head for her home port.

Fishery skirmishes and wars are increasing as more nations compete with each other for the fish of the sea. In the minds of many fishermen, they are exercising the mandate of God: "And God said, let us make man in our image, and after our likeness: and let them have dominion over the fish of the sea, and over the fowl of the air, and over the cattle, and over all the earth. . . ." Even when it pits man against man.

The world demand for seafood increases each year. Some nations consume more fish and fish products than others. Those that do have developed very aggressive fishing industries. At the present time, Japan and the Soviet Union are the most organized and technologically efficient of the fishing nations. Not far behind them are Great Britain, Peru, and the Scandinavian countries. The United States, although a major sea power, has a relatively small and less proficient fishing industry that has been allowed to deteriorate over the past quarter of a century.

So competitive is modern sea fishing that a number of nations have been forced to extend their territorial waters farther out to sea. Iceland has declared a fifty-mile limit. Peru claims two hundred miles as her limit. Other nations have limits in between these two distances.

United States territorial waters extend only twelve miles out to sea, although American fishermen are asking for a two-hundred-mile limit.

One important reason why American fishermen want to extend the fishing limit is that, in addition to a depleted fishing fleet, they must contend with heavy competition from foreign trawlers. Fishing boats from Bulgaria, Spain, Japan, and the Soviet Union flock to the fertile euphotic zones over the continental shelf in the North Atlantic. As a result of the heavy fishing, stocks of haddock, yellow-tailed flounder, and herring have been drastically reduced in the waters over Georges Bank, a part of the continental shelf.

Georges Bank is in the sea region that begins about seventy miles offshore of southern New England. New England fishermen claim that not only do foreign trawlers reap great harvests of fish in the waters over Georges Bank but damage the fishery grounds in the process. Marine communities on the bottom of the sea have been severely disturbed by the dragging of huge nets on the sea floor. Also, foreign trawlers take the small feeder fish with fine-meshed nets and, by doing so, further cut into the stocks of food fish by reducing the potential supply of large fish.

While admitting that the New England fishery industry is in serious difficulty, the United States Government has proceeded cautiously and slowly on the matter of extending American territorial waters to the two-hundred-mile limit. Even though New England fishermen want the two-hundred-mile limit, other fishermen and some government agencies do not. For example, the tuna and salmon fishermen oppose the extension of the territorial waters. Also, the American State Department opposes it.

Why this opposition to extending our territorial waters? The tuna and salmon industries think that if the United States does extend the limit, other nations will take retaliatory measures. Tuna and salmon fishing is conducted in pelagic (or open) waters. These two fishing industries are afraid that any extensions of territorial limits would reduce their fishing areas.

As for the State Department's opposition, its view is that the matter of territorial waters should be handled through international negotiations. This view was on the American agenda at the United Nations Conference on the Law of the Sea held in Caracas, Venezuela, in the summer of 1974. The United States also favors what is known as the species approach to the management and harvesting of fish. This approach provides for first rights to coastal nations to fish stocks found along and off their coastlines. In short, these nations would have first choice. Other fishing nations would have the right to harvest what was left without depleting the stocks. Coastal nations would also have regulatory control over fish stocks for as far offshore as the fish may swim.

Naturally, there is opposition to this concept. First of all, enforcement will be difficult, even impossible under certain circumstances. Secondly, such an approach would, in effect, give exclusive ownership of anadromous or migratory fish—such as steelhead trout, salmon, and striped bass—to the particular nation in whose waters these fish spawn. It is not difficult to understand why some nations (and fishery industries) oppose this approach to regulating world fishing.

It was the hope of the United States and other concerned nations that the Law of the Sea Conference would solve many of the sea's problems, especially that involving territorial waters and open sea fishing activities. In fact, the basic purpose of the conference was to draft an international treaty for the wise development and equitable sharing of the fish of the sea and other ocean resources among all nations. Yet even though the conference lasted for more than two months, no major decisions were reached other than to meet again in 1975.

Unquestionably, there must be international agreement and cooperation if we are to continue harvesting fish from the sea. Some fish stocks are close to the danger point for species populations. It is just one more step before these endangered species will be shoved into extinction.

Jacques Cousteau, the distinguished oceanographer, has said that "in ten years there will not be any fish remaining to take out of the ocean." In Mr. Cousteau's opinion, the rate at which the sea is being robbed of fish and fouled by pollution will soon force severe changes in the future harvesting of marine resources. There is sense in what Mr. Cousteau says, for we have but to consider this fact: we keep taking from the sea without putting anything back.

The sea's potential for producing an abundant supply of fish and shellfish is great. It is not possible to make a direct head count or population census of all the living marine resources, as has been done in the case of some terrestrial wildlife. All that can be accomplished is to estimate the fishery resources in different regions of the sea. Such estimates are being made by the Department of Fisheries, Food and Agriculture Organization, of the United Nations. This world agency is compiling data on the estimated total potential harvest of living marine resources for various parts of the world seas.

In each of the sea regions surveyed, the catches and potential supplies of living resources are divided into four main groups. One group is dimersal or bottom-living fish, such as cod and sole. Pelagic or open-water fish include sardines, herring, tuna, anchovy, and salmon. Crabs, shrimp, and lobsters are among the creatures that make up another group, the crustaceans. The fourth group, the cephalopods, includes the octopus and squid.

Many of the fishery resource sites now being surveyed by the United Nations Department of Fisheries are heavily fished. Some fish stocks were found to be overexploited, others underexploited. The survey made one fact absolutely clear: The overexploited fish stocks need immediate protection and sound management if they are not to become extinct. This need for conservation and regulation applies to open-sea stocks as well as those found in waters over the continental shelves.

The matter of possible extinction for some fish stocks cannot be taken too lightly. There is no question that the Atlantic salmon's precarious position today is a result of mismanagement.

ATLANTIC SALMON

Once, the Atlantic salmon *(Salmo salmar)*, or the leaper, as the ancient Romans called this magnificent fish, had an extensive range. When early man first migrated into Europe, the Atlantic salmon frequented the rivers and streams of Iceland, Denmark, England, Ireland, Scotland, France, Germany, Poland, Spain, Switzerland, the Netherlands, and the waters of the Baltic Sea; it was found in waters north to the Arctic regions; in Russian waters, eastward to the Pechora River; it abounded in Greenland waters and westward to the rivers of Canada and the northeastern United States.

This once populous migratory fish has an interesting life cycle. It begins life as roe or eggs placed in sand or gravel in cold rivers and streams. The eggs are laid by gravid (pregnant) females that have migrated in from the sea. The eggs remain in the beds for about eighty days in temperate regions and up to one hundred and eighty days in Arctic waters. Then they hatch into small fingerlings called alevins. Eventually, the young salmon reach what is known as the smolt stage and start their movement toward the sea. When they leave their native streams, they run a gauntlet of hazards. As they swim toward the sea, the young salmon are exposed to predators, pollution, dams, waterfalls, millraces, and power boats. Many of them do not make it to the sea.

The migration of young Atlantic salmon to the sea is not a continuous journey. That is, they do not make a nonstop, beeline course to the sea. Instead, their migration takes place in stages and with all kinds of interruptions, some of which prove fatal to the sea-bound salmon.

Actually, little is known about the transitional stage of *Salmo salmar's* life from the rivers and streams into the sea. It is possible, according to some authorities, that the salmon tarry a while in the brackish waters of estuaries to acclimate themselves to an oceanlike environment before entering the open waters of the sea.

Even though natural hazards took an annual toll of young salmon and adults, man's predation and activities were the chief factor in the decline of this fish. Agricultural and industrial development, in both the New and Old Worlds, played a major role in the destruction of Atlantic salmon habitats in Europe, Scandinavia, the British Isles, and North America. Dams and weirs impeded the travels of salmon to and from the sea. The lowering of water levels in rivers and streams for agricultural irrigation purposes, increased lumbering activities, and paper pulp manufacturing operations all contributed to the decline of the Atlantic salmon habitats.

In North America, the Atlantic salmon began to disappear from northeastern rivers in the late nineteenth century. New England factory activities, a reduced flow of water, lumbering in Maine, and unregulated fishing soon sent the number of salmon into a sharp decline. By 1880, only a few rivers in Maine and eastern Canada contained any appreciable stocks of *Salmo salmar*.

True, the Atlantic salmon ran risks in the open sea. At first, the pelagic or open-sea fishing of the Atlantic salmon was moderate. The main reason for this was that for many years, large schools of the salmon were rarely seen. Nobody knew where the Atlantic salmon went after they left the rivers. Once they entered the sea, they simply disappeared. Fishermen had to be content with small catches.

Then, in 1964, some Greenland fishermen discovered what turned out to be a major feeding ground for salmon. This feeding ground was in the Davis Strait off the west coast of Greenland. The discovery proved disastrous to the Atlantic salmon. As was to be expected, fishing fleets of a number of nations quickly converged in the Davis Strait. Now the Atlantic salmon was subjected to heavy hunting made easy by the use of sonar. With the aid of sonar devices, salmon fishermen had little difficulty in locating the salmon and catching them in nets or on hooks.

Salmon fishing in the Davis Strait was so heavy that a

sharp decline in the number of salmon reaching the spawning grounds was noticed by those nations possessing salmon habitats. Regardless of the drop in spawning salmon, the open-sea hunting went on year after year. The annual catch of Atlantic salmon in the Davis Strait soared from sixty metric tons a year to more than two thousand metric tons.

In the face of such intense hunting, the inevitable result was a steep drop in the catches of salmon in the open sea. To further aggravate the salmon situation, a new feeding ground was discovered in the Atlantic Ocean north of the Lofoten Islands, off the coast of Norway. And, as in the case of the Davis Strait feeding grounds, fishing fleets sailed to Norwegian waters to net the salmon.

In the 1960s, as the Atlantic salmon stocks continued to decline, most fishing nations reduced their salmon-fishing operations. Only one nation, Denmark, owner of Greenland, persisted in taking large numbers of the hard-pressed salmon, ignoring the requests of other nations to help conserve this declining species. The Danes pushed aside all protests, maintaining that the threat to *Salmo salmar* was exaggerated. Danish fishing companies denied any responsibility for the decline of the salmon in the spawning rivers of Europe and North America. They claimed that natural migration hazards caused the decline in salmon stocks and not Greenland fishermen.

An important factor in the Atlantic salmon controversy was whether salmon from European and North

American rivers migrated to the Davis Strait. If European and North American based salmon did not migrate to Greenland waters, then Denmark was right; Greenland fishermen were not responsible for the decline of Atlantic salmon in the rivers of Europe and North America.

In an effort to find the answer to this question, marine biologists in Europe and North America tagged hundreds of thousands of smolts, parrs, and adult salmon. Metal or plastic tags were inserted in the abdomens of the fish or fastened near their dorsal fins with wire. Many of the tagged fish were caught by fishermen. Most important, Atlantic salmon netted by Greenland fishermen carried tags placed on them by biologists in Canada, England, Ireland, and Scotland.

Here was ample proof that Atlantic salmon migrating from rivers in the British Isles and North America ultimately arrived in the feeding grounds in the Davis Strait. Yet, despite this evidence the relentless harvesting went on. The situation was the same in Norwegian waters, where salmon from the British Isles and Europe were harvested in large numbers. In 1969, the Danish salmon fishing fleet alone netted more than three million pounds of Atlantic salmon.

When the Atlantic salmon seemed threatened with extinction, a number of nations, including the United States, banded together in an effort to save this fish. An American conservation group, the Committee on the Atlantic Salmon Emergency (CASE), called for a total ban on the open sea fishing of *Salmo salmar.* This organization petitioned the International Commission for the Northwest Atlantic Fisheries (ICNAF) to take immediate steps to protect the salmon. CASE spokesmen pointed out that netting salmon in their feeding grounds definitely reduced the numbers that migrated back to spawn in their native rivers.

The Danes, also members of ICNAF, vetoed the proposed ban. On raged the controversy. Finally, a compromise was worked out: the next year's catch of Atlantic salmon would remain at the previous year's level. This measure would reduce catches, but it was a poor conservation program for a species already in danger of extinction.

Most of the conservation-minded nations objected to the compromise and soon CASE members demanded a boycott of Danish goods. They stressed the fact that the success of Atlantic salmon restoration in the United States depended upon salmon returning to North American rivers from the Davis Strait. The Danes were unimpressed by these and other arguments and went on taking salmon, asserting their legal rights to fish in the open sea.

Gradually, more and more nations looked with disfavor on the stand taken by the Danes. The United States became a leader in the fight to save the Atlantic salmon. In 1970, the United States Congress passed a law that became known as the Pelly Law after its sponsor. It authorized the President of the United States to restrict fish imports from nations believed to be harming or flouting international fishery conservation programs.

Also, Canada and the United States issued a joint statement that called for a total ban on Atlantic salmon fishing in international waters.

The United States imports nearly eighty percent of the fish consumed by Americans, including fish and fish products from Denmark. Therefore, the probability that exports of Danish fish to the United States would be halted caused the Danes to reconsider their stand on the Atlantic salmon. Late in 1971, they reluctantly agreed to limit their annual harvest of salmon to 800 tons, starting in the summer of 1972. The Danes also assented to a complete phase-out of salmon fishing by 1976. Greenland, as a Danish protectorate, would also limit its seven-year average salmon catches within its territorial waters to about 1,100 metric tons.

That is the way matters stand with the Atlantic salmon today. *Salmo salmar* is still being hunted in the open seas, in spite of waging a struggle for survival as a species. Many conservationists are disappointed with the rate of reduction for salmon harvests. They assert that the Danes should have agreed to a fifty percent reduction in the first year of the agreement rather than the twenty-one percent. Had the Danes done so, say some conservationists, they would have convinced the world that they are genuinely interested in conserving the fast-dwindling stocks of Atlantic salmon. In the eyes of many nations, a fleet of more than 300 Danish trawlers dragging eighteen-mile long drift nets to take a seriously endangered species is no magnanimous concession or laudable example of conservation.

The story of salmon-fishing points out only one specific example of mismanagement; many other fish stocks are in jeopardy. Yet, it does illustrate clearly that the increased harvesting of endangered fish and the intense competition for others cannot continue without serious consequences. World fisheries experts believe that only a small annual increase in catches above present levels can be expected in the future, even with conservation measures. When the stocks of primary food fish give out, then we shall have to turn to other less desirable species.

All nations, developing or established, must realize that the right to fish in the open seas does not include the right to exterminate species. Each nation has a moral, if not legal, responsibility to help conserve the sea's living resources. Man's dominion over the fish of the sea includes a trusteeship for protecting the supply of fish. To do otherwise is to invite the ultimate loss of a most valuable food source.

·5·

Plight of the Porpoises

"Farewell, thou faithful, friendly fish. Would that I could reward thee. But thou canst not wend with me nor I with thee. Companionship we may not have. May Galatea, Queen of the Deep, accord thee her favor—and thou, proud of the burden, draw her chariot over the smooth mirror of the deep."

Thus, according to Greek mythology, did Arion speak to the dolphin that saved him from drowning. Arion had been kidnapped by pirates and carried far out to sea. Rather than be killed by them, Arion jumped into the sea. His situation was desperate, for he was in deep water and far from the shore. He struggled to keep afloat. Finally, he stopped struggling and slowly sank beneath the waves. Suddenly a friendly dolphin came to his rescue. The dolphin buoyed up the drowning man and towed him to the shore.

There may be those who will dismiss this episode as mere myth, at most, an imaginative tale not to be taken seriously. True, the story of Arion and the dolphin is a myth. But the friendliness and helpful behavior of dolphins and porpoises are based on fact. Both in historic and recent times, accounts of dolphins and porpoises holding up exhausted swimmers in the sea or bumping them out of dangerous riptides have been recorded and documented.

Many ocean bathers and sea travelers have watched the agile and graceful antics of a school of dolphins or porpoises. Their playfulness and intelligence are well known to many people who have visited one of the large aquariums or aqua-stadiums that feature performing dolphins. For centuries, these interesting sea creatures were thought to be large fish. Then, in the eighteenth century, Carolus Linnaeus, the Swedish botanist who founded the modern system of taxonomy or classification of animals and plants, declared all dolphins, porpoises, and whales to be mammals. He placed them in a special order known as the *Cetacea*. Dolphins and porpoises are small whales.

Despite Linnaeus' classification, many people still regarded them as large fish. Herman Melville, author of the American classic novel, *Moby Dick*, insisted that the whales were fish, scientific evidence to the contrary. "Be it known, waiving all arguments," wrote Melville in 1851, "I take the good old-fashioned ground that the whale is a fish, and call upon Holy Jonah to back me up."

Today, of course, most people know that whales, dolphins, and porpoises are marine mammals. As for the dolphins and porpoises, there are some differences between them. These are mainly scientific and not easily apparent to the layman. The term *porpoise,* in common usage, is generally used to designate both dolphins and porpoises. However, zoologists throughout the world apply the term *porpoise* to members of a specific genus, the *Phocaena.* To avoid confusion, both dolphins and true porpoises are included in the term *porpoise* in this book.

Marine biologists and animal behaviorists have amassed a store of knowledge about the habits and behavior of porpoises. Most studies on them have been conducted in sea-environment aquariums, such as the Marineland of the Pacific Research Laboratory, the New

PORPOISE

COMMON
DOLPHIN

York Aquarium, and the Naval Marine Laboratory at Kaneohe Bay, Hawaii.

The intelligence of porpoises, their friendliness to human beings, and their willingness to perform various tasks and tricks have made them popular with scientists and the general public. These are some of the reasons why many people are disturbed over the slaughter of porpoises by Japanese fishermen and the American tuna industry. Thousands of porpoises die each year. Approximately twenty thousand are taken by Japanese fishermen and supposedly used for food. Nearly two hundred thousand porpoises die in the purse seine nets of American tuna fishermen. While the Japanese claim to eat porpoises caught by their fishermen, those killed in tuna nets are simply tossed back into the sea to be consumed by predators and scavengers.

Many Americans and several conservation organizations have called for a boycott of Japanese goods as a means to halt the taking of porpoises for food. Naturally, the Japanese object to the proposed boycott and Japanese fishermen oppose any ban on the harvesting of porpoises. Some Japanese officials emphasize that seafood, including porpoises and whales, has been a staple in the Japanese diet for hundreds of years.

Japanese fishery experts claim that a total ban on porpoise hunting is not necessary for the conservation of these small whales. If the present world catches of porpoises are not increased in the years ahead, according to Professor Masaharu Nishiwaki, world renowned cetologist, the populations of hunted porpoises will not be endangered.

Professor Nishiwaki stresses the fact that there is no indication of a population decrease when one looks at the number of smaller-size porpoises harvested; what this means is that if more small porpoises were taken, then it could be assumed that larger or older porpoises were becoming scarce because of overhunting. Also, according to Professor Nishiwaki, there has been no increase in the capture of fertilized females or even sexually mature porpoises in the annual harvests of Japanese fishermen. Still, the Professor believes that porpoise-harvesting should be closely monitored for signs of any population decrease.

The noted cetologist and other Japanese think it unfair for Americans to ask the Japanese people to change their food habits. Some nations, including Japan, simply do not have large supplies of protein food or adequate sources of beef, lamb, or pork. These nations must supplement their food supplies by taking food from the sea.

Professor Nishiwaki contrasts the Japanese use of porpoises with that of the wanton waste of these sea mammals by American and other tuna fishermen. He considers the waste of porpoises trapped in tuna nets a prime example of industrial disregard for marine mammal conservation.

There is truth in Professor Nishiwaki's contentions. Americans, by way of their tuna industry, are wasting a most valuable marine resource. Therefore, censuring the Japanese for killing porpoises and whales is hypocritical in view of the slaughter of porpoises in tuna nets. And calling for a boycott on Japanese goods is an unfair tactic. Tuna fishermen kill ten times as many porpoises as the Japanese, yet Americans are not boycotting the products of the tuna industry.

Five major American tuna canneries and a number of independent companies operate about 132 fishing boats that sail from southern California ports. These boats head for the waters of the eastern Pacific Ocean and the great schools of tuna. More ships will be added to this fleet, for tunafish is a popular and profitable seafood in the United States.

Tuna fishing is a very competitive business, not only between nations but between companies and even individual boats. Captains of tuna boats make every effort to locate schools of tuna and take as many as possible, regardless of any side effects of their fishing activities.

Imagine that you are aboard a tuna boat. A lookout is perched high on the mast. He shades his eyes and peers out over the sea, searching for signs of the valuable fish. Suddenly he leans forward in stiff attention. Dead ahead is one of the signs he has been seeking: a cluster of seabirds. The birds wing in and out of the water.

"Tuna ahead!" sings out the lookout.

The tuna boat captain calls for more speed and the boat plows through the choppy sea, bearing down on the area of bird activity. As the boat nears the site, you see porpoises leaping and flashing in the sunlight. They are the spotted porpoise *(Stelella graffmani)* and the spinner porpoise *(Stenella longirostrus)*, two species that follow schools of the yellowfin tuna.

As you stare down at the sea, you notice a dark mass in the water below the darting and leaping porpoises. This mass is the school of tuna. A motor boat is launched. It speeds in a wide circle around the porpoises and school of tuna, towing a half-mile-long purse seine net.

The motorboat completes its mission and both porpoises and tuna are encircled by the net. You watch as the net is drawn together around the porpoises and tuna. Most of the porpoises are on the surface; the tuna are below them in the net that is tightening around them, much in the manner that one closes a purse bag by tightening the drawstring.

Many of the trapped porpoises panic. They dash into the sides of the net in a frantic effort to escape. Some of them are caught in the mass of tuna and are slowly being smothered. Distress whistles fill the air. Other porpoises, loyal to their companions, dive down into the mass of tuna to help trapped porpoises. Then, they too die as the great mass of tuna presses down on them.

While you watch, hundreds of porpoises are hauled up with the tuna catch. Some porpoises manage to escape from the net, and these lucky individuals speed away from the disaster area. One or two of them break out of the water in long, flying leaps. Some cast a look backward as though conveying a farewell to their dead companions in the nets. Then the escaped

porpoises submerge and disappear in the sea.
Only the hungry seabirds and sharks remain at
the massacre site.

You make a rough estimate of the dead
porpoises. Four hundred. Four hundred little
whales killed in the tuna catch. Then, as the
bodies of the dead porpoises are heaved into the
sea, you shake your head and wonder why it
had to happen this way.

Porpoise slaughters are all too common in the Pacific
waters where the yellowfin tuna run and men go out to
catch them. Few fishermen think twice about the dead
porpoises, for among all living creatures, those that live
in the sea are given scant pity.

Perhaps it is the harsh realism of a fisherman's life that
makes him callous or indifferent to the death and waste
of so many porpoises. He sees hundreds, even thousands,
of fish hauled up in nets. The fish flop around for a few
minutes, their gills sucking in and out and their tails
whipping back and forth. Then they die. The fisherman
gives them little attention, for he sees many mass deaths
at sea.

Even the amateur fisherman, whether fishing in fresh
water or in the sea, soon becomes accustomed to the
death of his or her catch of fish. Little pity is wasted on
the dying fish. Sometimes a fisherman hastens the death
of a fish by clubbing it. Most of the time the fish simply
expires. Porpoises may still be fish to many fishermen,
just as any hawk is a chicken hawk to a poultry farmer,
and their death occasions no lamentations.

Fortunately, many humanitarians and conservationists deplore the death of the porpoises. Public indignation over the slaughter of porpoises in tuna nets prompted the United States Department of Commerce—the agency that regulates commercial fisheries—to investigate the matter. An *ad hoc* committee was appointed to look into the killing of porpoises in the tuna nets. This committee examined the methods employed by fishermen to catch tuna and also considered alternative methods that might save porpoises trapped in nets. One suggested alternative was a modified tuna net devised by Harold Medina, a tuna boat captain.

Captain Medina invented his net modification in 1970. What he did was to fashion a section or panel that could be attached to an ordinary purse seine net. The panel consisted of netting with a smaller mesh than that in the regular purse seine net. The object of the panel was to facilitate a technique known as backing down, that is, a maneuver that lowered one end of the net.

The Medina panel, about five hundred fathoms in width and length, is fastened at the rear of the purse seine net, or that part furthest from the tuna boat. When the net is filled with tuna and porpoises, the boat maneuvers in such a way that the float line and panel at the back of the net sinks below the surface of the sea. This action permits porpoises to swim over the panel and out of the net. Tuna, swimming lower in the water and closer to the boat, do not escape. In tests at sea, the Medina net reduced the average porpoise mortality by seventy-five percent.

Unhappily for the porpoises, not all tuna boats are equipped with the Medina-type net. Nor are they compelled to have such a net. The use of the Medina net is strictly optional. Many tuna boat captains do not want to pay the extra cost of modifying their purse seine nets and therefore continue to catch porpoises.

Other types of porpoise-saving tuna nets are in the experimental stage. A two-section net—one that will hold tuna at the bottom while porpoises above can be freed—is being tested at the Northwest Fisheries Center in Seattle. This net is 102 feet long and has a mid-purse line located 70 meshes below the corkline.

The net works as follows: when the purse line is drawn in and the pursing operation completed, two distinct or separate nets or bags result; one below the other. The tuna remain in the lower bag, while the porpoises go to the top. The top is opened, and the porpoises swim out. Then, the middle purse line can be released, and the net used in a normal manner.

The Commerce Department's *ad hoc* committee made other recommendations. These included a cooperative federal-tuna industry program geared to instruct fishermen in the use of the backing down technique to save porpoises. Also recommended were a general improvement in tuna-fishing gear, research projects on the behavior of tuna and porpoises in nets, and a population estimate of porpoises.

Provisions of the Marine Mammals Act of 1972 stated that tuna fishermen must revise their fishing techniques and adopt methods that would protect porpoises from being trapped and killed in nets. The law set a deadline of October 21, 1974, for a halt in the killing of porpoises in tuna nets. At the expiration of the deadline, the killing of porpoises must be reduced to insignificant levels or, better still, entirely eliminated.

As in the case of other industries forced to adopt measures to protect the environment and natural resources, the tuna industry has protested controls on their activities. Fishermen, like farmers, are fiercely independent and object to being told what they may or may not do.

Ordinarily, the right to conduct a business as one sees fit—providing no laws are violated or any harm done—is a traditional American right. But the tuna industry has been killing porpoises, a natural resource that belongs to all peoples of the world. While tuna fishermen have been granted the right to take tuna in international waters, they have not been given the right to kill thousands of porpoises. Since they do kill porpoises, accidentally or otherwise, they should be held accountable. They should not resent or try to block programs that will help them avoid large-scale slaughter of a valuable marine resource, even though such slaughter is an unavoidable side effect of their tuna operations.

Tuna industry spokesmen have told a Congressional panel that the October 1974 deadline could not be met. They stated that unless the deadline was extended and the United States began to employ sanctions against other tuna-fishing nations, the survival of the American tuna industry would be in grave doubt.

In mentioning sanctions against other tuna-fishing nations, the spokesmen were alluding to a provision of the Marine Mammals Act of 1972. This particular provision authorizes the Department of Commerce to place embargos on imports of fish and fish products from nations that fail to meet American marine conservation standards. Tuna industry officials claim that the United States is making no sincere effort to apply this provision. Nor is the United States, according to tuna fishermen, even seeking cooperation among foreign nations through negotiations and agreements.

Unquestionably, the protection of porpoises is an international concern. Most of the troubles of the sea are global in distribution, and solutions require the cooperation of all nations using or depending upon the sea. The American tuna industry can be a leader in putting into practice conservation and management programs that will help to save a most important marine resource: the porpoises. But for one reason or other, most tuna boat operators have not taken this important step.

While boycotts are distasteful measures and no cure-all for a problem, more and more people are leaning toward them as a way of forcing industries and nations to protect the ocean environment. It is a trend that the tuna industry should keep in mind if it wants the American people to continue to buy its products. The industry should not take refuge behind loopholes in the laws or threaten the reduction or cessation of tuna fishing because of having to comply with conservation measures.

Charley the tuna needs a better image. Instead of

telling television viewers that his company wants only the best tuna in the sea, he ought to be telling them that his company is taking quality tuna from the sea without killing porpoises. Or, at the least, he should tell them that his company is working to devise methods and equipment that will *reduce* the number of porpoises caught in tuna nets.

Some boycotts against tuna products are already in effect in the United States. The Greenwich, Connecticut, Board of Education voted in 1972 to ban tunafish in its school cafeterias. This boycott will continue until the slaughter of porpoises in tuna nets is stopped or at least greatly reduced. In Pennsylvania, a school district outlawed tunafish in its school lunch programs. Other groups are considering similar bans against tuna products.

What most Americans want in the long run are international regulations that protect the sea and its living creatures. They want fishery industries to conserve dwindling fish stocks and reduce the accidental death of porpoises. They want other industries, agriculture, and municipalities to stop polluting the ocean environment. They do not want laws, such as the Marine Mammals Act, which read as though a great deal is being done to protect the ocean environment, when, in reality, very little is being done.

Above all, people want conservation laws and regulations that have no loopholes through which industries can wriggle. In the case of the harassed porpoises, the people want the tuna industry to proceed with alacrity.

They believe American tuna fishermen should cooperate with other nations, scientists, and fishermen to employ all possible means to save porpoises. The friendly and intelligent porpoises are too valuable a resource to be wantonly destroyed by negligence, especially when the means to reduce losses are available.

Certainly Japanese fishermen should reassess their operations and harvests of porpoises for human consumption. They should not take more than is needed, and, even then, they should pay heed to protecting breeding stock and rare species. Perhaps the time will come when American and Japanese fishermen, like the Russians, will cease killing porpoises and regard them, as the Russians do, as the "marine brothers of man."

·6·

Titans of the Sea

"Thar she blows!"
"Where away?"
"Three points off the starboard bow."
"How many?"
"Six. And thar go flukes!"
"Lower away all boats!"

It was in this manner that nineteenth century whalers out of Salem and New Bedford reacted to the sighting of the great sperm whales. Whaleboats were hastily lowered into the heaving sea. Harpooneers balanced themselves in the bows of tossing boats, their harpoons or irons poised for the lethal toss into a whale. Oarsmen bent their backs to the oars, sending the whaleboats dashing against the buffeting waves toward the whales wallowing just ahead.

The nineteenth century was the golden age of whaling, and the ships of many nations put to sea to chase and capture the leviathans of the ocean. Whaling, in Herman Melville's time, narrowed down to a struggle between the largest and strongest mammal on earth and puny man, armed only with a harpoon and superior brains. Many men died in pursuit of the whales. Boatloads of them were hurled into the sea, where they drowned or were crushed by whales.

Melville spent four years aboard whaling ships, and in his book, *Moby Dick*, there is this description of whalers making contact with a whale:

> "A short rushing sound leaped out of the boat; it was the darted iron of Queequeg [chief harpooner on the whaling ship, *Pequod*]. Then all in one welded commotion came an invisible push from astern, while forward the boat seemed striking on a ledge; the sail collapsed and exploded; a gush of scalding vapor shot up nearby; something rolled and tumbled like an earthquake beneath us. The whole crew were half-suffocated as they were tossed helter-skelter into the white curdling cream of the squall. Squall, whale, and harpoon all blended together, and the whale, merely grazed by the iron, escaped."

Whaling today is, of course, less hazardous than in Melville's time. Superior ships and equipment, as well as hunting techniques have eliminated much of the danger in capturing these great sea mammals. Modern whaling, unlike that of the nineteenth century, is a blend of science and technology. Whalers utilize fast boats, aircraft, and sophisticated navigational equipment to locate and capture whales. Against these, even the strongest and speediest of whales has little chance of escape.

Modern whaling is dominated by Japan and the Soviet Union, with Peru, Norway, Canada, Great Britain, Iceland, Argentina, France, South Africa, and Australia joining them in the competition. The United States, once the greatest of whaling nations, no longer hunts whales. In addition to ceasing its whaling activities, the United States bans the importation of all whaling products.

In the nineteenth century, the main objective of the whaling industry was to capture whales for their oil and baleen, the peculiar bristlelike structure found in the heads of certain whales known as baleen whales or *Mysticeti.* Whale oil was in great demand as an illuminant for lamps. Baleen was used as support material in corsets and other foundation garments. But it was the oil, the most profitable of whale products, that lured hundreds of whalers out of Salem, New Bedford, and other ports of the world.

Even though whale oil is no longer in great demand for its illumination qualities, it is still sought because new uses have been found for it. For example, it is used as a base for oleomargarine in some countries. Some nations use whale oil as a lubricant.

Most nations hunt whales for meat and other by-products. Japan and the Soviet Union claim they must hunt whales to supplement the food supply of their peoples. Consequently, Japan and the Soviet Union take the major portion of the world whale harvest, about eighty-five percent of the catches.

These and other whaling nations employ techniques and gear that were not even dreamed of in Herman Melville's whaling days. Picture, if you will, a modern whale hunt. A pod of sperm whales is sighted by observers in a helicopter. Now a high-speed boat chases the whales. A whale-scaring machine aboard the boat—a device using ultrasonic noises—stampedes the whales, forcing them into rapid flight. The boat and helicopter follow, staying with the frightened mammals until the creatures become exhausted and fall victim to the chase boat with its high-powered harpoon guns.

When the whales are killed, they are towed back to gigantic factory ships. The equipment and crew aboard the factory ships are capable of dismembering the whales and rendering their parts into oil and other products. These factory ships are costly to operate, and their owners make every effort to keep them busy processing whales all during the hunting season.

Because of intense hunting, the stock of whales has been steadily declining since the nineteenth century. First, whalers depleted the population of Arctic right whales in the waters near Spitzbergen, Greenland, the Davis Strait, and in the Pacific Arctic waters. In the temperate seas, the black right whale gradually disappeared, first in the northern hemisphere, then in the southern. Right whales, so-called because whalers regarded them as the right whales to catch for high profits, soon were classified as a rare species that is present throughout their ranges in small numbers.

Next, the gray whale, a common species seen in the waters off the California coast, began to lose ground, and it, too, became a rare species at the beginning of the 20th century. When these two species became scarce, whalers turned to the speedy blue, finback, and sei whales. These whales were the main species hunted and processed by factory ships after 1925, when the Arctic seas were opened to whaling.

By the late 1930s, whale oil production reached the highest peak in history. Oil processed from the catches of more than forty factory ships exceeded 600,000 tons. This oil was obtained from more than 40,000 whales, most of which were the giant blue whale, the largest mammal ever to live on earth.

Each year, the hunting of whales increased, and the stocks of blue whales, along with those of sei, fin, and humpback whales, went into a sharp decline. As a consequence of the rapid drop in numbers of these whales, some whaling nations agreed to limit their catches in the Antarctic sea, particularly for the fast-disappearing blue whales.

But these agreements, with their difficult-to-supervise regulations, failed to halt the decline of the whales. There were several reasons why they failed to do so. One was that there was no organization—national or international—to supervise whaling activities and enforce regulations. Another was that not every whaling nation agreed to limit its annual harvest of whales. A third reason was that little was known about the life cycles, behavior, and migration of the whales—vital information needed for conserving and managing the cetaceans.

After World War II, the commercial attack on whales shifted from the rare blue to the fin whales. Then the familiar hunting pattern was repeated: Year after year, the whalers reaped large harvests of the fin whales, cutting into the populations. As a result of overhunting, whaling nations soon noticed a sharp decline in fin whale stocks.

Again, concerned nations called for regulations on whaling methods and catch quotas. At the invitation of the United States, a number of whaling nations sent delegates to an International Whaling Conference held in Washington, D.C., in 1946. An important development of this conference was the establishment of the International Whaling Commission or IWC, as it is known. The IWC was given authority to set harvests limits in the Antarctic Sea and prescribe whaling practices for member nations.

The IWC also designated a portion of the Pacific region of the Antarctic Ocean as a whale sanctuary. This sanctuary still exists. It may be opened or closed to whaling, according to the authority vested in the IWC. The IWC can stipulate the minimum body lengths at which different whale species may be taken. In this matter, the IWC acts much in the way of a state fish commission that sets the minimum size for freshwater fish. Also, the IWC defines the duration of whaling seasons and specifies areas outside the Antarctic region where factory ships may or may not operate.

Other whale conservation and management measures are the responsibility of the IWC. One is the protection of nursing females and their calves. Another is that the IWC has the authority to extend protection to endangered species (ones whose chances for survival and reproduction are in immediate jeopardy), such as the blue, sei, and humpback whales, and to rare species, such as the arctic and black right whales and the gray whale. Equally important, the IWC has the authority to supervise the utilization of harvested whales. That is, the IWC can insist that whalers eliminate wastage by processing the entire whale—meat and bones, as well as oil. Some whalers hunt and process whales just for one or two products, wasting the remainder of the whale's body.

Various scientists advise members of the International Whaling Commission. They are mainly biologists with a knowledge of whale stocks, geographical ranges of whale species, migration habits and routes, breeding capacities, age ranges, and population dynamics. Unfortunately for the whales, the IWC has not always heeded the counsel of its scientists. If it had listened to them in the 1950s, stocks of southern blue and fin whales would not be at their present all time low numbers.

Some critics contend that the IWC favors the whaling industry in matters of catch quotas and whaling practices. Others charge that the IWC is actually a cartel dominated by two of its most aggressive whaling nation members: Japan and the Soviet Union. And by catering to these two whaling nations, the IWC, according to critics, is not a responsible international agency for the conservation and management of a rapidly diminishing resource of the sea.

There is truth in these accusations. The IWC must consider the interests and needs of a huge industry that deals in large amounts of money, ships, and labor. Perhaps a more fundamental weakness of the IWC is that it lacks the power to enforce its regulations. Regardless of reasons, the fact remains that despite catch limits and other regulations established by the IWC, at least eight species of whales are now classified as rare or endangered.

Bowhead whales *(Balaena mysticetus L.)* head the list of rare species, and their number is estimated at two dozen.

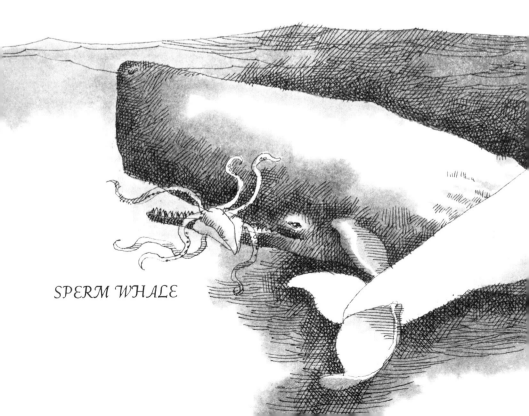

SPERM WHALE

The Atlantic right whale *(Eubalaena glacialis Borowski)* and the Pacific right whale *(Eubalaena sieboldi Gray)* have been so reduced by hunting that their numbers may be counted in the dozens in a few remote regions of the sea. The great blue whale *(Sibbaldus musculus L.)*, a species that attains a length of one hundred or more feet, has dropped in numbers from about 100,000 a half-century ago to fewer than 1,000 today.

Endangered by overhunting is the boisterous, melodious singing whale, the humpback *(Megaptera novaeangliae Borowski)*. This knobby-headed whale emits melodic

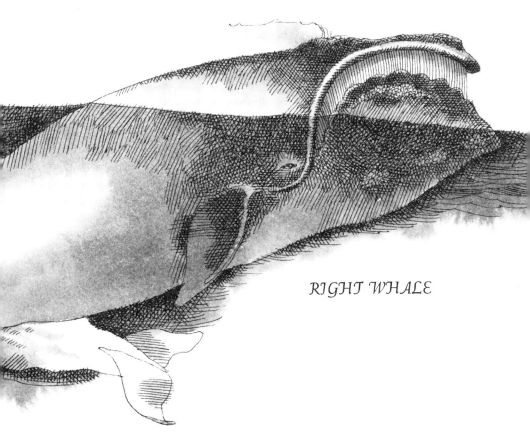

RIGHT WHALE

sounds, and its song was first recorded by Dr. Roger S. Payne in the sea off the Bermuda coast. The song of the humpback whale is a tuneful olio of sounds that remind one of a blend of the oboe, cornet, moog, and bagpipe.

Gray whales *(Eschrichtius glaucus Cope)*, often seen swimming off the California coast, have been protected for more than thirty years. These whales, once reduced to very low numbers, have slowly increased their populations. The number of the California group of gray whales is now estimated at ten to twelve thousand. But the gray whales that once frequented the waters off Korea have disappeared, undoubtedly as a result of overhunting. American scientists are now conducting research on the behavior and migration of the California gray whales.

Four other species of whales are now heavily hunted, and their numbers are declining each year. One of these is the finback *(Balaenoptera physalus)*, second largest of the baleen whales. It often reaches a length of eighty feet. Although it is a fast swimmer, the fin whale is losing the battle to maintain its numbers. Once estimated at more than 400,000 individuals, the population of fin whales today is now placed at 100,000.

The sei whale *(Balaenoptera borealis)* is the third largest of the baleen whales and grows to a length of sixty feet. Relentless hunting of the sei has cut its population in half. Formerly estimated at 150,000, the present number of sei whales is believed to be about seventy-five thousand. A close relative of the sei, Bryde's whale *(Balaenoptera edeni)*, which may reach a length of fifty feet, is also heavily hunted and suffering a decline in numbers.

Finally, the largest of the toothed whales *(Odontoceti)*, the sperm whale *(Physeter catadon)*, has been severely reduced in numbers. The sperm whale is an economically important species and reaches a length of sixty feet. It has a distinctive square head, diagonal spout, and rut-lined body. Sperm whales are the most cosmopolitan of all whales and are found in all of the oceans. These whales tend to group in harems lorded over by a large bull whale. Sperm whales feed on squid and will dive deep into the sea to obtain this food. Once estimated to number six hundred thousand, the present population is perhaps two hundred thousand individuals.

There is no question that the regulations and whaling practices established by the IWC have been ineffectual in halting the decline of these species. In the past twenty-five years, all commercially valuable whales have been subjected to a ruthless and relentless slaughter. The rate of killing whales today is far greater than that in any other period in the entire history of whaling. Where, in Herman Melville's day, whaling ships were lucky to take a whale a month, whales are now being killed at the rate of one every twelve minutes.

The tragic part of this slaughter is that, with a few exceptions, there is no real need for whale products. In the nineteenth century, the peoples of various nations demanded whale oil for their lamps, meat for food, skins for leather, bones for corsets, and other parts of the whale for various by-products. Today, there are excellent substitutes for all whale products except meat.

Whale meat is a nutritious food. It is rich in histidine,

lysine, arginine, fat, vitamin A (from whale liver), and other valuable nutrients. Histidine is an important factor in human nutrition, for it is essential to body growth. Also, meat from some whales (for example, the finback) contains no parasites transmissible to human beings, something that cannot be said of pork or beef.

Again, there is no question that whale meat is a nutritious food. What is questionable, in view of the sharp decline in whales, is overexploitation and mismanagement of this important sea resource by the Japanese and Russians. If these two nations are so dependent upon whale meat to feed their peoples, as they claim, then their wanton reduction of whales is puzzling if not irrational. They are killing off an important source of food, which, they say, they must have to supplement the diets of their peoples.

Renewable natural resources must be protected and wisely managed if they are to remain available. This is true in the case of timber and terrestrial wildlife. It is equally true for the whales and other living resources of the sea. Annual catches of whales should be geared to what is known as the maximum sustainable yield. This means that only those whales should be taken that can be killed *without endangering the ability of the species to sustain and reproduce itself.* Neither the Japanese nor the Russians are adhering to this time-tested natural resource management principle.

Of course, this principle, when applied to the harvesting of whales, will permit only moderate catches of some species. For example, because of their scarcity, the catches of blue, sei, bowhead, and humpback whales would be reduced to permit these species to increase their diminishing populations.

Japan and the Soviet Union would have to be content with smaller catches. But, to use an old cliche, half a loaf of bread is better than none. By following the maximum sustained yield principle, Japan, the Soviet Union, and other whaling nations would be ensured of a *permanent* supply of whales. That is something they will not have if they persist in their present whaling practices.

So far, Japan and the Soviet Union have ignored the appeals of other nations to conserve the whales. Japan has actually expanded its whaling activities. Japanese whalers are now hunting the Antarctic minke whale (*Balaenoptera acutorostrata*), smallest of the baleen whales that has an estimated population of no more than three thousand. Furthermore, the hunting of minke whales is in violation of IWC regulations, which permit the taking of only fin, sei, sperm, and Bryde's whales.

Much of the pressure on whale populations would be eased if the Soviet Union also reduced its whaling activities and abided by IWC quotas and regulations. It should be noted that the Russians ceased hunting porpoises because they believed these small whales were the "marine brothers of man." Apparently the Russians do not regard the large whales as their brothers. At least, Russian whalers do not consider the commercial whales as their big brothers.

World opposition to Japanese and Russian whaling practices and their flouting of IWC regulations is gaining momentum. Other nations, led by the United States, have asked for a ten-year moratorium on the killing of whales. Even among the Japanese people, there are those who think Japan should reduce her whaling activities and join the rest of the world in preserving the great sea mammals.

What is being done to make Japan and the Soviet Union realize that they are destroying a most valuable marine resource? Since IWC rules and regulations have been ignored by the Japanese and Soviet whalers, and officials of these two nations have dismissed protests of other nations, some powerful conservation organizations are calling for boycotts of Japanese and Russian goods. The demand for boycotts on Japanese goods has increased because of a recent report that Japan is exporting thousands of tons of whale meat in the form of pet foods and rations for ranch mink. The argument of some Japanese officials that Japan must hunt whales to help feed hungry people seems spurious in the light of evidence to the contrary.

The National Wildlife Federation of the United States has asked for a boycott on Japanese-made automobiles, cameras, electronic equipment, and clothing, and on Russian products, such as canned fish, alcoholic beverages, and furs. Also demanding a boycott of Japanese and Russian goods is the National Audubon Society. Spokesmen for this conservation organization said that its decision was based on the fact that neither the Japanese nor Russians would cooperate with other nations in preserving the supply of whales.

Many children of the world are concerned about the whales. A children's crusade to save the whales is winning many supporters in a number of nations. Three young girls (representing Canada, Sweden, and the United States) recently traveled to Japan with letters from more than 75,000 children, who urged the Japanese to stop killing whales.

The United States, once the most aggressive and relentless hunter of whales, is now the leading champion of these titans of the sea. But one nation alone cannot save the whales. The fate of the cetaceans is in the hands of all nations, but particularly those engaged in whaling activities. Unless these nations act in a responsible manner, the whales may soon follow other overexploited species into extinction.

In the last fifty years, more than two million whales have been slaughtered and converted into lubricants, pet foods, shoe polish, paint, soap, margarine, fertilizer, car wax, and machine oil. Yet there is no need to kill whales for these products; substitutes are available.

If we no longer need whale products, why worry about what happens to the big sea mammals? Why should the boy or girl in Kansas or other places far from the sea worry about what happens to the whales? Most of them have never seen a whale except on television or in a book.

True, we no longer need whale products. But that fact is no reason to abandon the whales and permit a few nations to exterminate them. Whales play an important role in maintaining the balance of the marine ecosystems. They are a major strand in the web of life. What happens to them can affect all other life in the sea. Besides, just knowing that whales will continue to swim in the sea is comforting to those of us who are disturbed and angry because of the many animals that have become extinct in the last one hundred years.

Therefore, each of us should try to hasten the time when the familiar cry of the lookout—"Thar she blows!" —will cause mariners and fishermen of all nations to aim binoculars at the whales, instead of high-powered harpoons.

·7·

The Fur Seals

St. Paul's Island in the Bering Sea. Although it is summer, a cool Arctic wind sweeps over the island and ripples its coastal waters. A male fur seal breaks out of the sea and flops onto the rocky slope of the island. It waddles awkwardly to higher ground and turns toward the sea, coughing hoarsely.

Now another bull seal surfaces in the sea, springs upward, and lands on the island. More bulls appear and join the vanguard. Soon the air is filled with challenging roars as the seals jostle each other for a position on the bleak slopes, competing for territories.

Later, the females or cows will arrive to deliver the pups they have been carrying for a year. Then the island that has been still and desolate will become active with life. The northern fur seals have once again returned to their ancestral breeding grounds in the Pribilof Islands.

For thousands of years, the northern fur seals have been making their annual migrations to and from the breeding grounds in the Bering Sea. Before the advent of man, their travels were endangered only by natural predators of the sea: sharks, killer whales, walruses, and ice-dwelling polar bears. Then man appeared and began to hunt the seals, first to provide necessities of life and then for profit.

The eighteenth century Russian mariner, Vitus Bering, pioneered the navigation of the frigid sea now named after him. He sailed his ships through the fog-enshrouded waters past the Aleutian Islands and on to the coast of Alaska. After Bering came hordes of Russian fur trappers—known as the promyshlenniki—eager to exploit the seals and sea otters in the waters of the Bering Sea.

These Russian fur trappers found the natives, Eskimos and Aleuts, accomplished hunters of the seals. Soon the Russian fur trappers had the natives working for them, catching the valuable fur seals and sea otters that abounded in the waters of the Aleutian Islands and the Alaskan coast. But the Russians did not pay the natives for the pelts; instead, they demanded a certain number of prime furs as payment for a tribute levied against all natives.

Russia, laying claim to the Aleutian Islands and Alaska, also imposed fur tributes on each vessel sailing to the Aleutian Islands or the Alaskan mainland. These tributes often amounted to one-tenth of the total fur catch per vessel. Then, when the Russian American Fur Company was established in Alaska, the exploitation of the fur seals entered a new, concerted hunting stage.

The coats of fur seals (pinnipeds) are quite unusual. The coats are dense, with a growth of fine, short hairs that provide these sea mammals with the necessary insulation to protect them from the icy waters. Between the short hairs are longer and coarser hairs known as guard hairs. The guard hairs are removed when the pelt of a fur seal is prepared for the fur market.

The unusual quality of the fur seal's pelt made it a highly prized skin and the demand for the pelts in America, China, Russia, Europe, and Japan in the nineteenth century caused seal slaughters that severely reduced the numbers of these mammals.

The role of the United States in reducing the fur seal population began before the purchase of Alaska from the Russian Tsar Alexander in 1867. American trappers and sealing ships swarmed to the Pribilof Islands and the Bering Sea to compete with other nations for the valuable seal and otter skins.

After the purchase of Alaska by the United States, one American fur company, the Alaska Commercial Company of San Francisco, was granted the sole right to take seals on the Pribilof Islands. This forced other sealing nations, mainly Russia, Japan, and Canada, to engage in pelagic sealing, the taking of migrating seals in the open seas. Since hundreds of seals were killed while migrating to the Pribilofs, the number returning to the rookeries was severely reduced each year.

The Alaska Commercial Company appealed to the United States to protect its rights to the seals. While the

United States Government could prevent sealers of other nations from taking seals on the islands, it had no legal right to stop open sea hunting of the seals. Nevertheless, it did try, ordering that all ships engaged in pelagic sealing in the Bering Sea be seized by the United States Coast Guard.

As a result of this action, a long and drawn out controversy over the rights to hunt seals occurred, reaching bitter proportions when some Canadian sealing ships were seized by United States Coast Guard patrols. The United States Congress enacted legislation that gave the American people dominion over the seal herds on the Pribilof Islands, but the State Department wisely ruled that pelagic sealing could not be halted by any unilateral action by the United States.

This seal controversy went on for a number of years. Finally, in 1893, the various nations engaged in sealing in the Bering Sea arrived at an agreement for controlling seal hunting and protecting the herds in the North Pacific waters. Yet, despite the agreement, the slaughter of fur seals continued. Enforcement of any regulations was difficult, if not impossible, in such a vast and remote expanse of water as the Bering Sea.

By 1910, the numbers of northern fur seals had been so decimated that the four major sealing nations realized that some protective measures would have to be taken. Consequently, the four nations sent delegates to a convention for the purpose of drawing up a new treaty that would protect the seals as well as the sealing rights of the four nations.

There were a number of major problems that had to be solved if the measures were to work. The most important was the question of jurisdiction over the fur seals. The seals were migratory mammals, moving in and out of the territorial waters of the four nations. Therefore, who owned the seals? Russia? The United States? Japan? Canada? The question of jurisdiction was an important one, and its solution would form the basis of any treaty to protect the seals.

Northern fur seals *(Callorhinus ursinus)* breed in summer and early fall on the rocky slopes of the Pribilof Islands in the Bering Sea. They also breed on the Commander

NORTHERN FUR SEAL

Islands beyond the western tip of the Aleutian Island chain and on Robben Island in the Sea of Okhotsk. Spring and winter find the seals widely dispersed in the waters of the southern Bering Sea, the North Pacific, the Sea of Japan, and the Sea of Okhotsk. The Pribilof Island herd winters in the Gulf of Alaska and in the coastal waters of British Columbia.

The prickly question of jurisdiction was eventually worked out by the delegates. Since the majority of fur seals occupied both American and Russian waters at different times of the year, these two nations would act as stewards of the herds. They would also conduct the killing of seals within their territories. But seals also migrated to the Pribilof Islands from Canadian and Japanese waters. Therefore, these two nations had some claim on the seals and were entitled to compensation.

The 1911 fur seal treaty prohibited open-sea hunting of fur seals. It allocated compensation to the four nations claiming rights to the seals. The United States and the Soviet Union would pay fifteen percent of the proceeds from all of their land sealing operations to Canada and Japan.

Then the matter of Japan's fur seal operations was worked out. Japan would pay the United States, Canada, and the Soviet Union ten percent of the proceeds from the land harvesting of seals in Japanese territories. Canada had no land sealing operations for the northern fur seals and therefore was not required to make any payments to the other nations.

This treaty also established measures and regulations

for conserving and protecting fur seals from overhunting by sealers from any nation. It lasted until 1941, when the Japanese bombed Pearl Harbor and entered into a war with two nations that were signatory members of the fur seal treaty, Canada and the United States. Most of the Japanese fishing and sealing fleets were destroyed during the war and little sealing was done by Japan. After the war, Japan rebuilt both fleets. When she did so, she engaged in more aggressive and technological fishing, sealing, and whaling operations.

The next twelve years brought temporary and weakly enforced programs to protect the fur seals. Few people outside of those involved in the fur trade even thought about seals. Most Americans did not even know what was happening to the seals on the Pribilof Islands or even where the islands were located. Arguments between the sealing nations became more heated and sealers from all four nations that were signatory members of the 1911 treaty violated conservation and regulation programs.

Finally, the four major sealing nations met again in 1957 to draw up a new treaty. Under the terms of this treaty, the northern fur seals could be hunted by the signatory nations but under strict controls aimed at preserving the Pribilof Island herds.

Disagreements and violations notwithstanding, the fur seal treaties of 1911 and 1957 have enabled the seals to rebuild their populations. Once at an alarming low number because of overhunting, the northern fur seal population is now at a high enough level to lift the seals out of the endangered species status. Officials of the four major sealing nations point to the fur seal treaties as an example of international cooperation for the conservation of wildlife.

While the fur seal treaty is still in force, there are certain flaws in the present seal management programs. One problem that concerns wildlife biologists is that the ratio of males to females is out of line in the total seal populations. Twice as many males are being killed as females in the annual harvests.

All of the Pribilof Islands are set aside as a fur seal sanctuary. Each year about eighty percent of the three- and four-year-old bulls are killed for their pelts, oil, and by-products. The total annual kill amounts to about 60,000 bachelor males and 30,000 surplus females of various ages. This rate of harvesting the seals, according to wildlife specialists, is not supposed to affect the species population in an adverse manner.

But is this true? Some biologists think not. A survey of the fur seal population dynamics shows an imbalance in the reproduction rate. Also, there is evidence that most females ovulating for the first time are not being bred. Female seals formerly ovulated at the age of three years, at which time they were usually bred. Now, for some reason, the breeding has slowed down. Biologists believe that it is less than in former years.

Why the reduced reproduction among the fur seals? Scientists do not have the answer at the moment, but there are some speculations as to the causes. For instance, Professor Nishiwaki thinks that inadequate controls over the seal catches may be responsible for the changes in reproduction among the fur seals. It may be that too many males are being killed. Other biologists and wildlife managers think that a combination of factors is involved; for example, pollution, killing of too many males, and disturbances in the seal habitats by speedboats and other human activities.

Undoubtedly, the overkilling of males is a major factor in this particular problem. The catch quota of the northern fur seals is decided each year by the signatory nations to the seal treaties: Canada, Japan, the Soviet Union, and the United States. It is based on the number of seals, estimated partly by direct observation of the herds and partly by a theoretical calculation as to seal numbers. Whatever the method of figuring the number of seals, the harvest is kept to the calculated maximum yield that will not adversely affect the total seal population.

Another flaw in the seal management program, and a major one as far as humanitarians and humane societies are concerned, is the method of harvesting the seals. While most people are unfamiliar with the population dynamics of the seals or the reproduction problems, they are acutely aware of the manner in which the seals are killed. Television documentary films showing the seal slaughters have aroused public sympathy for the seals and demands for more humane methods of killing them.

At harvesting time, fur seals on the Pribilof Islands are simply clubbed to death. It is this seemingly callous method of killing that enrages a large segment of both the American and Canadian public. A leading opponent of these seal harvesting methods is the Humane Society of the United States. Spokesmen for the HSUS point out that marine mammal protection bills now before Congress call for a five- to ten-year moratorium on the killing of marine mammals, but exclude the fur seals.

Former Secretary of Commerce Maurice Stans, yielding to public pressure to investigate the seal killings, visited the Pribilof Islands in 1971. Mr. Stans witnessed the killing of seals on St. Paul Island, along with a team of American veterinarians. Later, a report was issued to the effect that the manner in which fur seals are killed was a humane method. This method, according to the team of veterinarians, amounted to what could be called a satisfactory euthanasia or relatively painless death.

The HSUS and many individual humanitarians do not agree with these findings. Frank J. McMahon, chief investigator for the HSUS, monitored the killing of fur seals for four years. He maintained that Secretary Stans and the veterinary team saw only a small sample of the annual seal harvest. Furthermore, in Mr. McMahon's opinion, the 1971 harvest was not a typical one since very few seals came to the rookery on St. Paul's Island during that particular season.

Mr. McMahon's point was that in view of the reduced number of seals on the island, the hunters were more careful in killing the seals. When the seals are at the rookery in full force, the hunters have to work at a fast rate and, as a result, have less time to kill the seals properly. During the height of the average slaughter, a number of seals are not killed outright because of hasty or sloppy techniques. Many of them are severely wounded and allowed to suffer for varying periods of time. It is this cruelty that offends the sensibilities of humane people.

John A. Hoyt, President of the HSUS, in testifying before the House of Representatives Merchant Marine and Fisheries Committee, stated: "It is our contention that this government, which on numerous occasions has declared humaneness to be a matter of public policy, should pursue with great deliberation, a more humane method of slaughtering seals."

By law, the United States Commerce Department has jurisdiction over the fur seals on the Pribilof Islands. This agency is supposed to protect and wisely manage the herds, entering into agreements with other sealing nations. Yet the Commerce Department is often in conflict with sound wildlife management practices. Traditionally, the Commerce Department has defended and aided commercial interests, often to the detriment of marine resources.

This placing of the control of natural resources in agencies that might have conflicting interests is a major snag in our overall conservation program. For instance, the Department of the Interior has the responsibility of protecting wildlife, including predators. Yet, in the past, it has yielded to vested interests and not only sanctioned the killing of coyotes, wolves, mountain lions, and bobcats, but actually aided and abetted the western states in predator control. In the case of the predators, the Federal Government, steward of wildlife, was engaged in destroying wildlife that rightfully belonged to all of the people.

Canada, conceding to public pressure, now rigidly regulates the killing of harp seals *(Pagophilus groenlandicus)* in the Gulf of St. Lawrence. Yet, seals in the Quebec area are still killed by a sharp blow on the head with a club. Canadian officials defend the seal harvest with the argument that the seals are overeating the available supply of fish, pointing out that the average seal consumes about a thousand times its own weight in fish in a year. Thus, it seems that seals and man are now competing for fish stocks depleted not by excessive seal populations, but overexploitation by greedy fishery nations.

The American and Canadian fur industries have been warned that the public will no longer tolerate the wanton and inhumane killing of seals. But the fur industries and sealers of other nations are not under any such strictures. Sealers of other nations persist in employing inhumane methods to kill seals. For example, baby harp seals are being clubbed to death in the Labrador region by Norwegian sealers. Each year, beginning in March, the clubbers collect their grisly harvest of seals.

Some southern seals, not previously subjected to heavy hunting, now face increased predation by man. At an international convention held in London in 1972, and attended by an American delegation, it was agreed that a total of 190,000 Antarctic seals could be harvested each year by various sealing nations.

Ironically, all of the nations participating in this seal

convention were signatories to a 1961 Antarctic Treaty. This particular treaty attempted to establish conservation measures for the Antarctic region. But the 1972 treaty seems to forget about conservation measures. Delegates to the 1972 treaty convention claimed that the setting of annual quotas for seal harvests were conservation measures; their argument was that the lack of any quotas would permit the taking of any number of seals.

Their argument is not only specious but a poor substitute for sound seal management programs. Actually, any quota is a target at which to aim and sealing nations will certainly push to fill their quotas. And they will do so regardless of the status of the seal populations.

Three species of seals are involved in the Antarctic sealing operations. They are the crab-eating seals *(Lobodon carcinophagus)*, which will account for 175,000 of the total seal quota; leopard seals *(Hydrurga leptonyx)*, making up 12,000 of the quota; and Weddell seals *(Leptonychotes weddelli)*, which account for 5,000 of the annual quota. There is a strong feeling among some conservationists that the British fur industry, which processes about eighty-five percent of the fur seal pelts in the world, was instrumental in getting the British Government to sponsor the Antarctic seal convention.

Other pinnipeds are seriously threatened by increased hunting. One of them is the hooded seal *(Cystophoroa cristata)*. The young hooded seals have the unfortunate distinction of possessing a fur that is more highly prized than that of baby harp seals. The world population of hooded seals is estimated at between three to five hundred thousand. The average kill each year is about seventy-five thousand, most of which are taken off Greenland, the chief breeding and molting grounds.

The gray seal *(Halichoerus grypus)* is also under attack by fishermen from the British Isles. This seal is persecuted because fishermen claim that it steals Atlantic salmon from nets. It is also thought to carry the codworm, a parasite that damages important food fish. A periodic culling of the gray seal herds (rarest of the world seals) helps to keep these pinnipeds under control. The present population is estimated at 50,000 individuals.

There are three main groups of gray seals which are distributed in the waters of the eastern Atlantic, western Atlantic, and the Baltic Sea. There are colonies on the Orkney and Shetland Islands, the Hebrides, the Farne Islands off the Pembrokeshire coast, and in Irish coastal waters. Many of the gray seals enter estuaries to feed on cod and salmon. They are very fast swimmers and difficult to shoot, according to fishermen who hunt them.

Gray seals have been protected by British laws since 1914. However, from time to time, open seasons are declared on gray seals when the populations increase too rapidly and they began giving difficulties to fishermen. In 1963, the British Government permitted fishermen to kill bulls, calves, and adult females as part of a five year plan aimed at reducing the herds. But the killings caused a public outcry and it was discontinued.

British fishermen are again asking that they be permitted to kill gray seals. They claim the seals are multiplying too fast. Some British biologists and ecologists believe that a limited reduction in the gray seal populations will not harm the survival rate of the species. Others disagree. There is a dearth of knowledge on the reproductive rates and overall ecology of all seals, including the gray. Irresponsible controls and mass killings by fishermen and hunters could seriously endanger the seals, particularly the rare species.

Certainly the protection now afforded seals should never be revoked. Controlled harvesting, as a wildlife management tool, is necessary from time to time. But the total lack of any protection or control will lead not only to overexploitation but cruelty in the methods of harvesting. Man and seals have managed to coexist since ancient times. There is no moral or scientific reason why they cannot continue to do so, today and tomorrow.

·8·

Sea Otters

Most of the world's wild fur-bearing mammals have experienced a violent relationship with man. Beaver, fisher, marten, mink, leopard, ocelot, jaguar, and fur seal have been heavily hunted for their valuable pelts. Each of these species has had its numbers drastically reduced by overexploitation, but none has been closer to extinction than the frolicsome sea otter of the northwestern coastal waters of North America. Highly prized for its prime fur, the sea otter was subjected to one of the most intensive extermination programs in the history of wildlife.

Sea otters *(Enhydra lutris)* are members of the weasel family or *Mustelidae* and spend very little time out of the water. They differ from other marine mammals in a distinct physiological way. Seals, sea lions, porpoises, and whales rely on layers of fat or blubber for insulation against icy waters. But not the sea otters. Instead of the layer of fat or blubber, the sea otter has a layer of air that is trapped among its long, soft hair fibers. This layer of air helps to keep the otter warm in the cold waters of the North Pacific and the Bering Sea.

The coat of a sea otter is loose and thick, stretching to a length of six feet or more in an adult. In fact, a closeup view of an adult sea otter makes one think of a person wearing a dress or suit several sizes too big. The slackness of the sea otter's coat in no way detracts from its beauty. In color, the fur is white close to the roots, sometimes silvery, and darkening toward the outer ends of the hairs. The overall effect is one of great luster and velvety sheen. Moreover, sea otter furs are always in prime condition, for this otter, unlike other fur-bearers, lives in a relatively stable climate and as a result does not have a winter and summer coat. Also, the sea otter's coat contains adequate oil to prevent it from becoming waterlogged.

Sea otter skins are among the most expensive of all furs and are highly prized by people in many countries. Once they were the furs preferred by royalty and the wealthy, especially in China and Russia, where they were chosen over fox, marten, and sable. The great demand for sea otter furs and the high profits derived from their sale were the motives that sent hunters and trappers from a number of nations out after thousands of these playful marine mammals.

For most of recorded history, the range of the sea otter extended from Lower California northward along the west coast of North America; the fog-draped waters of the Aleutian Islands; the Kurile and Commander Islands; and the coastal waters of the Kamchatka Peninsula. As a result of overexploitation and human

SEA OTTER

activities, the range of the sea otter has been greatly reduced today.

Sea otters, unlike seals, porpoises, and whales, are not migratory, nor are they aggressive territorial mammals. They are very docile and live in family groups that keep on good terms with their neighbors. The otters prefer the coastal waters near a rocky mainland or island, and they rarely venture far out to sea.

These sportive marine mammals obtain their food, which usually consists of mollusks, crabs, fish, and sea urchins, by diving to depths of more than a hundred feet. In the case of hard-shelled food, the sea otters resort to the use of what might be called a tool to help them extract the meat. Sea gulls open clams and mussels by dropping them on rocks. Sea otters find a rock, roll over on their backs, place the rock on their chests, and, using the rock as an anvil or chopping block, the otter slams the crab or mussel against the rock, breaking the shell and exposing the meat. Sea otters have large appetites, and they engage in this interesting food-gathering habit many times a day.

The docility of the sea otters, their great curiosity, and their habit of staying in waters close to shores have made them easy prey for human hunters. Although Eskimos, Aleuts, and other natives in the coastal areas of the North Pacific and Bering Sea hunted the sea otters, their predation did not threaten their survival. Then, in the eighteenth century, when the Russian trappers arrived in the Aleutian Islands, the Alaskan mainland, and northern California, the hunting of the sea otters was intensified. The Russian American Fur Company sent its trappers out after the prized skins of the strange sea mammals that floated on their backs in the tossing coastal waters.

Russian trappers, aided by Eskimos and Aleuts, killed thousands of sea otters and sent the beautiful pelts to Russia and China. For a time, the Russian American Fur Company had a monopoly on the sea otter trapping. Then American and Canadian trappers came to the sea otter habitats to compete for skins. British fur merchants also sought the otter pelts.

The British entered the lucrative sea otter trade by way of Captain James Cook's expeditions. Cook made two trips through the Bering Sea during which his ships stopped at Aleutian and Alaskan ports. Sailors from Cook's ships obtained sea otter pelts from Aleuts and

Eskimo trappers. Later, when the Cook expedition ships sailed to Canton, China, the sailors found merchants eager to buy the otter pelts.

Naturally, Cook's sailors were delighted with the offers to purchase their sea otter pelts and sold the pelts for a total sum of two thousand pounds, a large amount of money in those days. The sailors were astounded by their good fortune and many of them wanted to return to Alaskan waters to engage in the highly profitable sea otter trade. A number of them did so and managed to kill nearly five thousand otters in a relatively short time.

News of the profits to be had in the sea otter trade soon drifted around the circle of British businessmen in Canton. Then, in 1785, the first British commercial venture into the sea otter fur trade took place. Captain James Hanna sailed his ship, laden with British goods for barter, into Alaskan waters for the purpose of obtaining sea otter pelts. Both Russians and natives were anxious to trade with Hanna, and in exchange for his goods, he took aboard five hundred prime sea otter skins.

Captain Hanna was eventually followed by other British merchant ships sent out by the British fur industry. Each year, the competition for the pelts increased in scope and tempo. Even damaged skins brought a good price in China. This fact added to the troubles of the sea otters. Since they did not have to be careful about the condition of the otter skins, many trappers killed otters in whatever way they could—often in an inhumane manner. Why worry about how the animal was killed? An otter skin was salable even though it had holes or rips in it.

So heavy and widespread was the hunting of the sea otter by the British, Russians, Aleuts, and Eskimos that the stocks of otters in Aleutian waters were soon depleted. Therefore, the hunters moved to new hunting grounds: the coastal waters of the Alaskan mainland and southward along the northern California coast. Eventually, they were joined by American fur trappers.

American trappers and fur merchants came to the Bering Sea region after Captain Grey of Boston discovered the mouth of the Columbia River in 1792. Boston ships, following Grey's route, sailed around Cape Horn and up the California coast past the mouth of the Columbia River. From here, they entered Alaskan waters and competed for the sea otter skins.

These Boston ships carried British goods to be used in what amounted to a three-way trade. First, the goods were swapped for sea otter pelts. Then the ships sailed to China and traded the otter skins for tea, nankeen (a buff-colored, durable cloth woven in China), and other Chinese goods. Next, the ships sailed back to Boston and other New England towns, where the Chinese goods were sold.

This three-way trade proved exceptionally profitable to British merchants and ship captains. But it was a source of irritation to the Russians, particularly Alexander Andreyevich Baronov, Director of the Russian American Fur Company and Governor of Alaska. Baronov complained to American trappers and fur merchants about the taking of otter skins.

"We are a commercial people," one American told Baronov, "and we look for profits, and there is nothing to stop us from doing so." These were prophetic words, for they formed the basis of a credo that was used to justify the heavy exploitation of not only the sea otters, but many other species of wildlife in the nineteenth and early twentieth centuries.

So intense and competitive was the hunting of sea otters, that Baronov became uneasy about the situation. In a report to his associates in the Russian American Fur Company, Baronov wrote as follows:

> "Just recall this one fact," wrote Baronov in 1800, "for more than ten years, English and American ships have been visiting this coast at the rate of six to ten a year. They figure that if they take less than 1,500 otter skins, they encounter a loss. There are places along this coast where they will get 2,000 to 3,000 skins. Let us assume that the average is 2,000—with a minimum of six ships per year—12,000 otter skins will leave here. And even if you take a lower average, say 10,000 skins, the total will be 100,000."

Baronov was by no means a conservationist. Nor was his concern about the rate at which the otters were being killed based on any humane principles. His worry was a potential loss of profits for the Russian American Fur Company. His report emphasized that sea otters were being taken at a fast rate and that the Russian American Fur Company could expect a sharp decline in sea otter pelts in the near future. In those days, the sea otters had no protectors.

Baronov's predicted drop in the number of sea otter skins did occur as American, British, and Russian trappers kept plundering the dwindling stocks in the Alaskan waters. Even after the United States purchased Alaska from the Russians, the hunting of sea otters continued at a heavy rate. In the period between 1880 and 1890, more than 48,000 otter skins were taken by the Alaska Commercial Company of San Francisco alone. This company was also heavily engaged in sealing on the Pribilof Islands.

So relentless and widespread was the hunting of the sea otters, and so depleted their numbers, that trappers, in 1900, took less than two hundred skins. The sea otter supply was giving out. The sportive, friendly sea mammals were no longer seen in northwestern coastal waters. Rarely did anyone observe the once-familiar sight of a family of sea otters, floating on their backs in the icy water, cracking clams and crabs on rocks resting on their hairy chests.

Again, as in the case of the fur seals, it was commercial interests rather than conservationists that prompted action to halt the extinction of the sea otters. In 1911, the same year that the first international seal treaty was signed, Japan and the United States reached an agreement to help preserve the remaining sea otters in the North Pacific waters. Japanese trappers had found the stocks of sea otters dwindling on their side of the North Pacific and they were interested in doing something about the situation.

The new treaty offered protection to all sea otters north of the 30th parallel. It created a sea otter sanctuary for otters in which no hunting would be permitted. This safety zone extended from Lower California westward across the Pacific Ocean to southern Japan, and then northward into the Bering Sea. To protect sea otters further, Congress enacted a law making it illegal to sell sea otter pelts in the continental United States and the Territory of Alaska.

Wildlife biologists and conservationists welcomed the protective measures afforded the sea otters by the new treaty. Many of them expected the otters to make a rapid climb to higher numbers in their populations. The otters, though, did not make the expected comeback in numbers. Year after year, only a few otters were sighted and even after more than fifty years of protection, they still were a rare sight in the 1960s. The failure of the sea otters to rebuild their numbers puzzled wildlife specialists who scanned the coastal waters for signs of the mammals. The big question was: Would the sea otters join the ranks of extinct species?

Fall, 1965. A biologist sits on a rock along the Pacific coast near Carmel, California. He watches a group of marine mammals swimming in the gently billowing water. At first, he thinks the swimmers are seals or sea lions. He stares at them. Then he takes a long look at them through a telescope.

He notices that the mammals have flat heads, long tails, forepaws, and webbed hind-feet. Some of them float nonchalantly on their backs, bobbing up and down in the swell of the sea. A few appear to be asleep in this recumbent position.

The biologist can scarcely believe what he sees. Now he smiles and nods his head. He is elated, for the lazily floating mammals in the sea are no other than the rare sea otters. Quickly dismantling his telescope, the biologist rushes off to report his discovery.

Gradually, more sea otters appeared in the waters off the California coast and in the Bering Sea. When the California Fish and Game Commission conducted a census of sea otters in waters under its jurisdiction, it found that there were about three hundred of the mammals.

The sea otters continue to rebuild their populations, and their estimated number today is 50,000—a small number compared to their population in the eighteenth and nineteenth centuries.

Most wildlife specialists believe that total bans on hunting or harvesting of game and fur species are not sound management measures. A complete halt to the hunting of populous species would result in surplus animals that destroy a habitat's food and cover, thus exposing themselves to starvation. But there is no doubt that the ban unquestionably helped sea otters to rebuild their populations.

Today, while it may sound unreasonable to some people, a certain number of sea otters must be killed each year to control their population. There are approximately 30,000 sea otters alone in Alaskan coastal waters. This number, according to Alaskan wildlife specialists, is too large for the available habitats and food supplies. The otters are not killed because their present habitats do not contain enough water. What is scarce—and growing scarcer—is an adequate food supply to support the otter populations.

Sea habitats, like those on the land, have a limited capacity to support wildlife. When that capacity, known as the carrying capacity, is exceeded, when there are too many animals, then the habitat is destroyed and many animals die. This is a waste of a valuable wildlife resource.

This kind of situation now exists in the Alaskan sea otter habitats, according to the wildlife specialists. Therefore, controlled hunting of surplus sea otters is a necessity. Under the close supervision of wildlife biologists, from five to seven hundred sea otters are culled from the populations each year. These yearly harvests do not threaten the survival of the sea otters.

What does threaten them are some recent man-induced hazards. Chief among them is pollution. All kinds of pollutants, some of them transported to the Bering Sea from distant shores, endanger the sea otter food chain. Chemicals and pesticides, in particular, contaminate clams, crabs, mussels, and fish consumed by the otters.

Biologists are already familiar with the harmful effects

of chemicals and pesticides on other forms of wildlife. DDT has caused considerable damage to fish-eating birds. The bald eagle is an example of what harm DDT and other chlorinated hydrocarbon compounds can cause in the bird's physiology. DDT, ingested by the bald eagle through contaminated fish, upsets the bird's calcium balance. The result is that affected eagles lay eggs with soft or thin shells. The eggs invariably break when the eagles try to incubate them, and the embryos are destroyed.

Oilspills also threaten the sea otter. True, sea otter hair is naturally oily, but nature has provided the otters with just the proper amount. An excess, such as that which occurs from an oilspill, is quite another story. When hairs become dirty or are saturated with oil, the insulating capacity is impaired or even destroyed. A sea otter with an impaired insulating system can, after long exposure in icy water, die.

Another danger to the sea otters is the increasing competition for food from the sea. Fish, mollusks, and crustaceans are important food for human beings, as well as sea otters, and each year more and more Japanese and Russian trawlers enter the sea otter habitat regions to take fish and shellfish. The sea otters cannot compete on equal terms with these fishermen. Some trawlers are equipped with suction machinery that can pull up more shellfish at one time than all of the sea otters can catch in a month.

In view of the increased human fishing activities in Arctic waters, with an inevitable reduction in the supply of fish and shellfish, perhaps it may become necessary to reduce further the sea otter populations. Such future culling would not be a result of any boom in sea otter numbers, but rather because man is taking more seafood.

The gradual encroachment on sea otter habitats by tourists, sports enthusiasts, and other persons, especially those who cruise or race motorboats in coastal waters, is another hazard the sea otters face. Motorboats are particularly hazardous, for sea otters float on their backs while resting, sleeping, or cracking open clams and mussels. When they do assume the floating position, they can easily be run down by a boat or wounded by its propeller.

Some scientists think that the mere presence of human beings in or close to sea otter habitats is causing harm to the otters. Breeding colonies are disturbed by the closeness of people. It is possible that this kind of disturbance, added to pollution and reduction of food supplies, may result in a substantial decline in the sea otter reproduction rate.

On the positive side, the jaunty sea otters have made a most remarkable recovery in numbers after over a century of relentless exploitation. Once again, the otters are seen floating on their backs with nursing young or cracking clams and mussels. Yet there is no room for complacency. There are new dangers for the sea otters, for some of the other troubles of the sea have spilled into sea otter habitats, endangering their lives, reproductive cycles, and food supplies.

·9·

Decline of the Sea Cows

In 1774, William Bartram, the son of John Bartram, the gentle Quaker botanist of colonial Philadelphia, saw a number of animals unfamiliar to him as he traveled through the Carolinas, Georgia, and Florida. At a spring near the Little St. John River in eastern Florida, William examined the skeleton of an unknown animal. Later, writing in his famous book, *Travels*, he described this strange animal:

> "Part of the skeleton of one, which the Indians killed last winter, lay upon the banks of the spring; the grinding teeth were about an inch in diameter; the ribs eighteen inches in length and two and a half in thickness, bending with a gentle curve. This bone is esteemed equal to ivory; the Indians call them [the animals] by a name that signifies the big beaver. My companion, who was a trader in Talahasochte last winter, saw three of them at one time in this spring; they feed chiefly on aquatic grasses and weeds."

Bartram, of course, was writing about the manatee *(Trichechus manatus)* once a common visitor in coastal rivers in the southeastern United States. It was not, as the Indians believed, a big beaver but a marine mammal belonging to a small order known as the *Sirenia*. Some paleontologists and zoologists think the *Sirenia* are distantly related to elephants and that both evolved from a common ancestor in prehistoric times. Others believe the *Sirenia* are related to seals. Regardless of their origin or relationship to other mammals, the *Sirenia* are unique and rare mammals.

There are three families in the *Sirenian* order, one of which—Steller's sea cow—is extinct. The two living families include the dugongs and manatees. Dugongs inhabit the coastal waters of the tropical Old World, while manatees live along the coast and in coastal rivers of the southeastern United States, the West Indies, northern South America, and western Africa. Steller's sea cow once frequented the cold waters of the Northern Pacific and the Bering Sea and were first seen by members of the expedition led by Vitus Bering.

Steller's sea cows were heavily hunted by the Aleuts and Eskimos before the Bering Expedition entered Aleutian waters. Thus, these Sirenians—the least abundant of the marine mammals in the region—were already declining in numbers when the Russians arrived in the Bering Sea. When Russian sailors and trappers joined the natives in hunting the sea cows, these mammals simply disappeared from Aleutian waters. The last Steller's sea cow was seen by a Russian messboy aboard a ship in

Commander Bay in 1768. After that sighting, the sea cow or *kapustnik* (sea cabbage eater), as the Russian sailors called this mammal, was never seen again.

Only one scientist was fortunate enough to observe Steller's sea cow. This was Georg William Steller, a German naturalist with the Bering Expedition, after whom this extinct sea cow was named. Steller apparently studied the habits and anatomy of the sea cows after he and the crew of the Russian ship, *St. Peter*, were shipwrecked on what is now Bering Island.

While Steller and the sailors were sick with scurvy and other ailments and suffered extreme hardships from the cold and dampness of the island, they did have adequate food. In the waters off the island the sailors captured sea otters, seals, fish, waterfowl, and the strange, roly-poly sea cows. There was fresh water on the island, so thirst was not added to the other miseries of the shipwrecked crew.

Georg Steller was especially intrigued by the sea cows and collected various parts of their skeletons, storing them away for future study. He did write a description of these odd sea mammals, but his work has undergone so many translations (and changes) that what remains cannot be said to be Steller's actual work. Unfortunately, Steller died after reaching Siberia on his way home from the ordeal on Bering Island.

But it is with the living families of Sirenians that we are concerned today. The extinction of Steller's sea cow by overhunting is lamentable. However, it is an accomplished fact, and nothing that we can do will ever bring this species back to the sea. Steller's sea cow suffered a fate from which the two remaining families must be spared.

One of the families is the dugong. The dugongs are relatively docile sea mammals that live alone, in pairs, or in small groups up to six or seven individuals. They feed on a variety of algae and aquatic grasses. When eating grasses, the dugongs rip out the entire plant, swishing it back and forth in the water to remove any sand or soil. They often pile stacks of plants on the shore close to the water, more or less as a larder. Later, the dugongs return to eat the plants.

Dugongs are very sensitive mammals, and any noise, above or below them in the water, easily frightens them. They have poor vision, and their inability to identify objects at a distance adds to their nervousness. Yet the dugongs, like the manatees, have a strong curiosity and they will try to examine objects in the water, including scuba divers.

Australian natives hunt dugongs for food, taking advantage of a physical peculiarity of this sea mammal as an aid in capturing it. Dugongs do not breathe in the same way as other sea mammals. They inhale quickly and then a special valve shuts off their nostrils. This mechanism enables the dugongs to remain submerged for varying lengths of time. What the Australian aborigines do is to enter the water and plug the nostrils of the dugongs to prevent the valves from opening later on. The result is that the dugongs die from asphyxiation, and all the aborigines have to do is to collect the bodies.

A single species of dugong *(Dugong dugong)* inhabits the Red Sea, the waters of the east African coast, the coastal waters around the Bay of Bengal islands, the Malay Archipelago, the waters of the Molucca or Spice Islands (Indonesia) to as far north as the Philippines, New Guinea, and the Australian coastal waters north of the tropical line. It is a warm-water sea mammal, restricted to the coastal waters, never entering fresh water or venturing far out to sea. In general, the geographic distribution of the dugongs depends upon the availability of aquatic grasses.

It is quite possible that in ancient times, dugongs provided the basis for the myths and legends about mermaids. Ancient sailors—at sea for as long as several years—returned home with stories about fishtailed women who lived in the sea and who could be seen basking atop rocks on isolated islands.

Shakespeare mentioned the mermaid in *A Midsummer Night's Dream*. In Act II, Scene 1, Oberon speaks to Puck:

> *"Once I sat upon a promontory,*
> *And heard a mermaid, on a dolphin's back,*
> *Uttering such dulcet and harmonious breath,*
> *That the rude sea grew civil at her song;*
> *And certain stars shot madly from their spheres,*
> *To hear the sea-maid's music."*

To sailors at sea for long periods of time, away from their homes and families, it was not difficult for them to imagine that the plump dugongs were women who lived

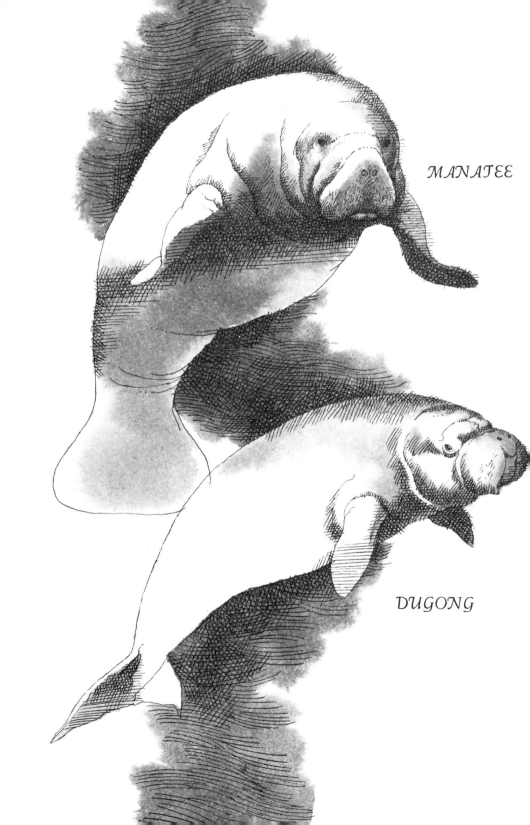

MANATEE

DUGONG

in the ocean. However, it is doubtful that the sailors ever saw dugong-mermaids on the shores or rocks or islands. Both dugongs and their close relatives, the manatees, are practically helpless on land and incapable of any locomotion when out of the water.

To return to the dugongs of today, this sea mammal is heavily hunted throughout its entire range. The dugongs, like other marine mammals, are sought for their valuable oil, which is rendered from their ample blubber. Hunters take them with various weapons, such as guns, spears, and clubs. Dugong flesh is used for food and the skin is turned into leather. Madagascar natives make a fine powder from the upper incisor teeth of the dugong, pulverizing the teeth by pounding them with rocks. The powder is used as a medicine that is supposed to cure persons sick from eating contaminated food.

The other living Sirenian family, the manatees, is more familiar to Americans since one species *(Trichechus mamatus latirostria Harlan)* inhabits coastal waters of the southeastern United States. This manatee is found in the waters off the Florida coast, the edges of the Everglades National Park, occasionally in the waters of the Florida Keys, the coastal waters of the West Indies, and off the coast of northern South America.

In United States territorial waters, the manatees exist in small numbers and in areas dominated by man. For example, they are found in the heavy boating regions of Biscayne Bay, the Miami River, and in the coastal waters north of the St. John River near Jacksonville, Florida.

The other two species of manatees are distributed in

the drainage areas of the Amazon and Orinoco Rivers in northeastern South America, and in the waters of West Africa, from the Senegal River south to the Cuanga River, and in Lake Chad. All three species of manatees are struggling for survival in most parts of their ranges.

Manatees have fusiform or spindle-shape bodies, with their forelimbs modified into flippers. They have no hindfeet but are equipped with a tail that has a rounded fluke. There are stout bristles on the upper lips of the manatees, and there are also short, stiff hairs scattered singly, like those on a pig, over their rotund bodies. This sparse hair gives manatees the appearance of being hairless. Manatee colors range from a dull gray to black.

There are no accurate estimates of the numbers of these harmless vegetarians of the sea. Since they are very shy and solitary, it is difficult to observe them in their natural habitats. However, a number of scuba divers, including marine scientists from Jacques Cousteau's research ship, have studied manatees under water.

The decline of the North American species has prompted the United States Department of the Interior to classify this manatee as an endangered mammal. As an endangered species, the manatee is not supposed to be harmed or killed.

Still, manatees are exposed to many hazards that are quite capable of harming or killing them. The risk of injury or death is high because the manatees frequent waters where man's activities and pollution are at high peaks. Unfortunately, the manatee's curiosity often leads it into danger.

Manatees will inspect all objects in the water, including motorboats equipped with death-dealing propellers. Some manatees are sliced by the boat propellers, others are simply run down by speedboats while they wallow in warm, shallow waters. Often the only indication that a speedboat operator has of the presence of a manatee is a sudden upwelling of water in the path of the boat and in most cases, the boat operator does not have time to swerve away. If not killed right away, the manatee sinks or dives to the bottom, where it may lie wounded and stunned. If it is mortally wounded, it eventually dies and is consumed by sea scavengers.

Although the United States protects the manatees in its waters, the same species is hunted for its oil, flesh, and skin in other parts of its range. The excellence and high quality of manatee flesh make this sea mammal a major source of nourishment for natives. Many of the natives living in the range of the manatee rely on this mammal in much the same way that the Aleuts and Eskimos depend upon seals, fish, and whales.

Unfortunately for the dwindling manatees, there are also a few so-called sportsmen who hunt them. These hunters do not kill the manatees for their flesh or oil but merely for the pleasure it affords them. They cannot even be equated with the big game hunters who kill Dall sheep, caribou, and other large mammals for the purpose of taking an animal with a large rack of horns or antlers, an ego-inflating act at best. Manatees offer no challenge for a hunting record (except in the number killed), and it is doubtful if one has ever been stuffed and mounted.

An increase in the numbers of scuba divers in Florida waters is another danger to the manatees. Some divers hunt the manatees in the rivers and shallow coastal waters. But their main threat is the disturbance of their family life. The divers disrupt the reproduction of the manatees, which usually mate in shallow water. Spectators, such as scuba divers, can seriously interfere with the mating process and later, with the rearing of the young manatees. Jacques Cousteau's fine documentary film about manatees in Florida waters clearly shows how manatees are disturbed by this kind of interference with their life cycles.

Of course, manatees, like other sea mammals, have natural enemies in the rivers and coastal waters. In the rivers, alligators and crocodiles kill very young manatees. Out in the coastal waters cruise the constantly hungry and eternally vigilant sharks. These large sea predators prey on young manatees, especially those that lag behind a group of adults.

Predation, in the sea and on the land, is a natural phenomenon. It is a factor that helps to control animal populations. Nature usually offsets losses by predators by increasing the reproductive rate of a prey species. Yet man has grossly interfered with this natural phenomenon. When man preys on wildlife, marine or terrestrial, he often kills many more individuals of a species than do the natural predators, such as wolves, lions, sharks, and birds of prey. As a result of man's heavy predation, nature's mechanisms for maintaining a balance in marine and terrestrial wildlife populations are thrown out of order. In the case of the dugongs and manatees, human predation of these sea mammals has caused far more damage to their populations than sharks, alligators, and crocodiles.

Since dugongs and manatees feed on aquatic plants in shallow water, any drastic alteration of their habitats and feeding grounds must also pose a serious threat to their survival. Coastal rivers and estuaries annually receive tons and tons of silt which piles up and encroaches on the aquatic plants so vital to the Sirenians. Other pollutants, such as chemicals, metals, and oilspills only add to the problems facing the Sirenians.

Although the United States protects its manatees from hunting, it has not been able to protect them from pollution and some of the other hazards mentioned earlier. Banning the hunting of these unique sea mammals is, of course, a major step in their preservation, but it is also imperative that their habitats be preserved and protected.

Obviously, in the face of siltation, pollution, scuba divers, speedboats, and other hazards, more marine sanctuaries are called for in various parts of the Sirenians' ranges. They need havens where they can be reasonably safe and carefully managed. Certainly, in those parts of the world where they form an important staple in the diets of natives, every effort should be made to regulate hunting and establish quotas. The principle of maximum sustainable yields is applicable to the Sirenians as well as whales and other sea mammals. Uncontrolled hunting, aided by pollution and other hazards, will ultimately send the dugongs and manatees down the same trail as that forced on Steller's sea cow.

It is not unrealistic to consider transplanting dugongs and manatees from highly dangerous areas to safer habitats. Similarly, they could be moved from regions of scarce vegetation to those abounding in the aquatic plants and grasses relished by the Sirenians. Artificial stocking of wildlife, while not a panacea for all management problems, is feasible for the manatees. It has been successful in the case of fish and a number of terrestrial wildlife species.

We would also do better to put these sea mammals to another use other than as food. They are prodigious eaters of aquatic plants, including unwanted plants such as the ubiquitous water hyacinth that grows in canals and rivers. Excessive growths of water hyacinths choke the waterways and their removal is laborious and costly.

In experiments conducted by Florida biologists, some manatees have been used for this purpose. They cleared canals, rivers, and irrigation ditches in Florida of the noxious water hyacinths. An important finding came out of this project: water hyacinths and other such plants grazed by manatees do not make as rapid a recovery as do those treated with herbicides or weed killers.

Perhaps this particular usefulness of the Sirenians will encourage more protection for them. Even those who feel that wildlife must have a practical as well as aesthetic use may eventually come to realize that the dugongs and manatees are potentially useful animals. When they do, perhaps more protection will be given to the besieged Sirenians in all parts of their ranges throughout the world.

·10·

Sea-going Turtles

Everyone, according to Dr. Archie Carr, noted authority on sea turtles, should witness the phenomenon of sea turtles arriving at a nesting site and laying their eggs. What makes this event so special is that the great turtles travel thousands of miles through the sea to reach their ancestral nesting sites. They are propelled there by the urge to reproduce their kind and are guided by some mysterious navigational system. But the migration and egg laying are not without danger to the turtles.

A sandy islet in the French Frigate Shoals near the Hawaiian Archipelago. On the beach not far from the water, a man crouches behind a sand dune. He stares out to sea. Suddenly he sees something poking up from the gently billowing water. At first glance it looks like a periscope. But as an inward surge of the sea moves the object toward the shore, a body appears below the upstretched object. The man nods in satisfaction. What he sees in the water is a big sea turtle.

Now the turtle is in shallow water, bumping and scraping the sandy beach like a grounding rowboat. It is a female green turtle, and she has come to the islet to lay her eggs.

She is on the beach now and glances cautiously about her. She sees and hears nothing to alarm her. Crawling awkwardly in the sand, she heads up the beach and away from the sea. Her movements are slow and laborious as she drags her three-hundred pound body over the warm sand.

Now she stops. She has found a suitable site for a nest beyond reach of the sea. Settling down in the wind-rippled sand, she begins the task of digging a nest. She uses her paddlelike feet as shovels, scooping sand from under her body. Her excavating is done with care and skill, for the nest is to be no ordinary crater in the sand.

The nest gradually takes form. It is flask-shaped; wide at the bottom and narrow at the top. There is a good reason for this odd shape. Her eggs must be protected from too much heat from the sun that beats down on the islet. Later, the hatchling turtles must also be guarded against extremes in temperatures. And both eggs and hatchlings must be safe from being washed out of the nest by flooding from the sea.

With the nest completed, the green turtle starts the process of depositing her eggs. She squeezes out three eggs at a time. She will not lay her entire clutch now. Later, at intervals of several days, she will return to the islet and lay more eggs until her clutch reaches one hundred.

The first stage in her egg laying is accomplished, and the big turtle carefully covers the cache of eggs with sand. Then she proceeds to erase all signs of the nest and eggs, camouflaging the site with more sand.

It is time for her to return to the sea for a respite. She crawls toward the water with great deliberation. She does not stop at the edge of the beach but enters the sea without looking back.

She disappears under a large billow of water and remains submerged. Then she reappears farther out in the sea. She will stay in the area and make several more landings on the sandy beach to complete her biennial laying of eggs. That has been her pattern for a number of years.

But this time there is a change. A fisherman drifting in a motorboat sees the huge sea turtle. He starts up the motor and steers the boat toward the swimming turtle. He quickly overtakes her and draws up alongside. He flings a large net down and under her body. She immediately sinks in the water but is trapped in the net.

The turtle is heavy, and the fisherman strains and grunts as he hauls her great bulk into the boat. He reaches down and with both hands pushes the turtle over onto her back. She remains upside down, paddle-feet waving in the air, for she is helpless and cannot turn over.

On the beach, the man behind the dune

watches as the motorboat speeds away. He comes from behind the dune, hurries over to the turtle's nesting site, and spreads a blanket on the sand nearby.

He rapidly scatters the sand from over the nest, now and then glancing nervously around the beach as though expecting somebody to be watching his illegal act. The turtle eggs are uncovered and the man places them on the blanket. He bundles up the leathery eggs, casts another furtive look about him and then moves inland and away from the beach.

Man's predation on the sea turtles and their eggs, along with that by natural predators, such as sharks, dogs, raccoons, and other egg- or turtle-eating animals, is a major reason for the decline in numbers of these giant reptiles of the sea. Added to predation is the encroachment of man and his activities on turtle nesting sites. Only a few major nesting sites remain in the Hawaiian Archipelago and Caribbean islands.

The catching of turtles in the sea and the robbing of their eggs are not recent events. They have been going on for a long time. For centuries, sea turtles, especially the green turtle *(Chelonia mydas)*, have been an important source of protein from the sea. Various island and coastal natives rely on the sea turtles for food and materials for utensils and ornaments. Turtle soup and steaks are the delight of gourmets everywhere and have been ever since English and Spanish fleets first sailed into Caribbean waters and the warm areas of the Pacific.

Naturally, the continued pressures on the sea turtle stocks have caused a decline in the numbers of most species of sea-going turtles. Commercial exploitation alone has reduced their populations to a point where some genera are actually endangered. The turtles are exploited not only for their food value, but for by-products used in the manufacture of exotic turtle jewelry, leather materials, and even certain cosmetics.

There are five genera of sea turtles: the Green *(Chelonia);* Hawksbill *(Eretomichelys);* Leatherback *(Dermochelys);* Loggerhead *(Caretta);* and the Ridley *(Lepidochelys).* All five are experiencing difficulty in maintaining their populations; some are threatened by extinction unless exploitation is greatly reduced and their nesting sites preserved against development by man.

Nobody knows just how many species of sea turtles are actually in the sea. Except for a few isolated research projects, such as those conducted by Dr. Carr of the University of Florida and George Balaz of the University of Hawaii at Manoa, there are no major sea turtle programs. As a result much of the habits, life cycles, and migrations of the sea turtles remains a mystery.

Sea turtles have not had the benefit of a large amount of concern and sympathy from the general public. Perhaps the sea turtles are not as appealing as other wildlife. Certain wildlife, marine and terrestrial, do arouse the sympathies of people and cause them to protest overhunting or inhumane slaughter. This has been the case with the whooping cranes, coyotes, hawks, eagles, porpoises, seals, sea otters, and whales. Many people from different parts of the world have rallied to the aid of these endangered animals.

However, the situation of the sea turtles has not, with the exception of the publicity given to the work of Dr. Carr and his associates, been given enough attention. Dr. Carr's fascinating book about sea turtles, *So Excellent A Fishe*, did present the plight of the sea turtles to those persons who bothered to read the book.

Sea turtles are an important living resource of the sea and they play a role in the marine ecosystems. But turtles, like other living resources, have been wasted and mismanaged through the past several centuries. Until Dr. Carr and the University of Florida's zoology department launched *Operation Green Turtle*, a project aimed at preserving the green turtles and their nesting sites, nothing was done to ease the desperate situation of the sea turtles. *Operation Green Turtle* has produced some vital data on this particular turtle and has enabled scientists to instigate some protective measures.

Operation Green Turtle involves turtles in the Caribbean region. The University of Hawaii at Manoa is conducting research on green turtles in the waters around the Hawaiian Islands. Green turtles in this region are also facing problems, the most pressing being a gradual decline in nesting sites. At the present time, only one major green turtle nesting site exists in the entire Hawaiian Archipelago: the small sandy islets at the French Frigate Shoals. These islands are located about 480 miles northwest of Honolulu and are the nesting sites

GREEN TURTLE

for ninety-five percent of the green turtles in this region.

The islets at the French Frigate Shoals have been designated as a sea turtle sanctuary. Some poaching on the turtles and the robbing of their eggs by natives does occur. Worse still many of the turtles, hatchlings and adults, migrate from the islets and swim into sea regions where they are not protected. Here, fishermen and turtle hunters take them.

Sea turtles in both the Caribbean and Pacific waters are subjected to many types of hazards. The turtles, relatives of prehistoric land reptiles, are especially adapted for life in the sea. Adult turtles are rarely in danger from sea predators, such as sharks. They are endangered by man. In the sea, the big turtles are hunted by men with nets, harpoons, and even guns; on land, they are flipped over on their backs or carapaces and left to die.

Female sea turtles—perhaps because of their evolutionary ties with the land—must come ashore to lay their eggs. Males do not leave the sea. The biennial or triennial trips to beaches to lay their eggs thus expose the female turtles to a wide variety of predators, not the least of which is man. While only man preys on the adult turtles, the eggs and hatchlings are eaten by a wide variety of birds and mammals, of which the most predaceous are gulls and raccoons. Those hatchlings fortunate enough to elude land predators must run the gauntlet of sea predators, which includes sharks, kingfish, and mackerel. Because of man and natural predation, mortality among hatchling sea turtles is high.

Out of the one hundred eggs laid by a green turtle, a certain number will survive predation by birds and mammals. When there is large-scale robbing of sea turtle nests, then the species—whether it be green, hawksbill, Ridley, leatherback, or loggerhead turtle—is in difficulty. And the overhunting of adult turtles in the sea further adds to the interference with nature's attempts to maintain adequate numbers of sea turtles.

Even though sea turtles are protected in some world areas, hunters and fishermen continue to take them on land and in the sea. Not all of the sea turtles are hunted for their meat. Some are taken for their shells and skins. For instance, hawksbill shells are highly prized by the so-called tortoise shell industry. Sea turtle shells are preferred to plastic imitations. The United States extends protection to hawksbill turtles by way of the Endangered Species Act of 1969. This law makes it illegal to import or sell jewelry made from the shells of hawksbill and other sea turtles.

A bad feature of sea-turtle hunting is that much of the reptile is wasted. Turtle hunters or poachers kill turtles for just the shell or only a relatively small portion of the meat. The remainder of the turtle's carcass is left on beaches for vultures and other scavengers or tossed into the sea. As far as turtle meat is concerned, there was a time when the turtle hunter had to bring a whole turtle to market. Now it is much easier. All he has to do now is to cut strips of cartilege from the bones of the bottom shell or plastron. These strips may weigh five pounds, but they are eagerly purchased by the makers of turtle soup. Neither the soup-makers nor hunters care what happens to the rest of the three-hundred-pound carcass.

In an effort to offset losses in hatchlings and adult turtles, the University of Florida's *Operation Green Turtle* provides for the transplanting of young turtles. Hatchlings are moved to new beaches in the hope that they will, when mature, return to these protected areas rather than to those open to pollution, development, and predation by poachers.

Green turtle hatchlings have been transplanted from Caribbean nesting beaches to protected sites in Florida. Some have also been taken to sanctuary areas in the Virgin Islands National Park and Buck Island Reef National Monument. The Buck Island Reef is a rare barrier reef in the Caribbean. Its waters are calm and free from sharks that might prey on the hatchlings and young turtles.

As in the case of transplanted terrestrial wildlife, a number of factors are involved in the success or failure of this conservation measure. The most important is whether transplanted young turtles will return to new regions rather than the sites from which they were taken. "In *Operation Green Turtle*," wrote Dr. Carr in his book, "the fundamental unknown is whether an unswerving attachment to an ancestral nesting site is inherited by the hatchlings—or whether they inherit only a tendency to become strongly imprinted by the physical character of the particular place in which they first enter the sea—and travel in ways that let them locate that place when they become sexually mature."

The problem of protecting the sea turtles is similar to that of some marine mammals, notably the seals and whales. Sea turtles, seals, and whales live for most of the time in the open sea—in international waters. At other times, they enter territorial waters. Sea turtles, unlike the whales, actually come up on land, thus complicating the matter of protecting them. Regardless, the protection of sea turtles, like that of the migratory marine mammals, is unquestionably a matter for international cooperation. One nation alone cannot save rare and endangered migratory marine species from extinction.

A sea-turtle sanctuary on the beach of one nation or its territories is but a conservation half-measure. Turtles and their eggs and hatchlings are safe only when they remain in sanctuary areas. When the turtles leave the beaches—

and they, like the Atlantic salmon, are lured into the open seas by some force—fishermen and poachers reap a harvest of turtles.

Perhaps complete cooperation among all nations to conserve and protect sea turtles and other living resources of the sea is an ideal that may never be achieved. There will always be those nations and persons that will not abide by any international agreements or conservation measures. Then what recourse is there? Employ economic sanctions against such nations? Ban the importation of all sea-turtle products? Perhaps these might help, distasteful though they may be in view of the world economic problems today.

What about artificially raising sea turtles as a way of preserving these reptiles and maintaining stocks? Is it feasible? Sea-turtle farming is being conducted under the joint auspices of the Caribbean Conservation Corporation, the National Audubon Society, and other conservation-minded organizations. One project is the rearing of green turtles in the southern Bahamas.

This sea-turtle farming project is still in what may be called an experimental stage. It is not yet at the point where it can be said to be practicable on any profitable or large-scale basis. There are some hurdles to overcome and problems to solve. Time, effort, and money, plus experience, are needed in sufficient amounts before any commercial success in sea-turtle farming can be achieved.

Any kind of marine-animal husbandry requires considerable experience, as well as trial-and-error methods, before it can be declared a practical industry. For instance, the development of our livestock and poultry industries was a slow process. Their present high scientific and technological levels were not attained in a year, decade, or even a century. Therefore, we cannot expect sea-turtle farming—or any kind of marine life farming—to be an instant success.

We have dipped our hands into only the surface of the sea's potential as a supplementary source for the procurement of food. Mariculture and sea-animal husbandry are not impossible dreams. The conservation and management of sea turtles and other marine animals are within our technological abilities. What is missing at the present time is international cooperation that will allow us to apply our wildlife management technology. Without international cooperation, there can be no proper management of the ocean environment and the great sea turtles.

When nations do come together in a cooperative program to protect and wisely manage the sea turtles—when all nations and their peoples respect treaties and regulations that limit catches and preserve marine habitats—then perhaps a green, leatherback, or hawksbill turtle may venture onto the sands of a beach without fear of predation by man.

·II·

Loners of the Arctic Ice Packs

Most people do not think of polar bears as marine mammals. Yet the great white bears do enter the cold waters of the Arctic seas and swim for long distances. Many of them are open-sea dwellers in that they live far out on floating ice packs in international waters. Even those bears that frequent the coastal landmasses remain close to the sea, wandering over vast territories.

The polar bear *(Thalarctos maritimus)* is nearly as large as the grizzly and kodiak bears. Zoologists say that it is a relatively recent species that evolved from the European brown bear. Polar bears are distributed around the North Pole, on the ice packs and coastal land areas of Alaska, Canada, Greenland, Norway, and the Soviet Union. The occurrence of these bears in a region depends on the availability of open water and an abundance of seals and fish, primary prey of the bears.

Polar bears, like grizzly and black bears, are wanderers, traveling great distances on land or over ice packs.

Some male polar bears living on ice floes have been transported thousands of miles during their thirty-year life-spans. Others roam for hundreds of miles over the tundra and icy wastelands of the polar regions. Most of the bears on the ice floes are males; females and their cubs remain on or close to the land where they can find food and shelter.

Fish and seals are the primary prey of the polar bears, but these mammals will also kill sea birds, Arctic hares, musk oxen, and reindeer. In summer, polar bears have been observed feeding on berries, various plants, and even algae. Often the food habits of the polar bears, particularly when they prey on hares, musk oxen, and

reindeer, bring them into conflict with man's interests. Eskimos compete with the big bears for the scant food supply in the frozen northlands and sea.

The white bears, like their relatives, the grizzlies, are capable of considerable speed on land. They can turn on a burst of speed that enables them to overtake a hare or reindeer. Their furry feet serve as snowshoes, allowing them to obtain good traction in the snow, and their sharp claws serve as cleats for digging into the ice. Polar bears are accomplished swimmers. Some bears can reach a speed of nearly four kilometers (about 2.4 miles) an hour in the rough water of the polar sea. These bears have great stamina and strength, even when wounded.

POLAR BEAR

Admiral Robert E. Peary, American discoverer of the North Pole, witnessed the amazing stamina of the polar bear in the icy waters of Melville Bay near Thule, Greenland, in 1886. Peary was aboard his ship, the *Hope*, with some Eskimos. The ship's captain carefully threaded the craft through the dazzling icebergs in the bay. Suddenly one of the Eskimos shouted: "Nannooksoah!" Peary and the others looked to where the Eskimo pointed to a large polar bear on an iceberg.

Then, as today, a polar bear on an ice floe presented a tempting target. Shots were fired at the bear. "The captain and I both chanced a shot at him," Peary later wrote in a magazine article, "and the captain's bullet grazed his leg, making him whirl away and disappear round a pinnacle of the berg. Circling the berg, we discovered him in the water swimming vigorously, and several shots were fired at him, one of which took effect, for he apparently collapsed completely. Yet a few moments later, he was swimming off again. . . ."

Overhunting, of course, is the main reason for the decline in polar bear numbers. The white bears have been the big game targets of hunters from Canada, Greenland, Norway, and the United States. Arctic natives depend upon the polar bears as a source of food, clothing, and other commodities necessary to sustain or ease life in the harsh environment of the frigid north-lands. Warm sleeping robes, mukluks (fur boots), and other articles of clothing are made from the creamy white pelts of the polar bears. The teeth and claws of the bears are fashioned into ornaments by the Eskimos.

Polar bear skins have always been highly prized by

people in many countries. In past centuries, European monarchs and members of royal families coveted the skins of the white bears. In Victorian times, it was considered fashionable, as well as a status symbol, to have a polar bear skin stretched out on the floor of a library or den. Naturally, the demand for skins sent hunters to the Arctic land masses and ice packs in search of the bears, even though the hunters knew that they would have to face a powerful and ferocious animal.

The ferocity and strength of the polar bear, along with its white pelage, have not deterred hunters. On the contrary, big game hunters have been drawn to the white bears, which seem to challenge either the ego or manhood of both Eskimo and foreign hunters. In addition to the physical challenge offered by the bears, victorious hunters came away with a white skin that might bring as much as seventy-five dollars a linear foot.

Undoubtedly, a white animal affects human beings in a different way than do animals of other colors. The Plains Indians revered a white bison and ascribed magical powers to it. In addition, the chief or brave who owned a white buffalo robe was a special person in the tribe. Herman Melville's brooding, half-mad sea captain, Ahab, was more than awed by the white whale, *Moby Dick*. He hated it and hunted this rogue whale in all of the world's seas, partly because it was white, but mainly because, in a previous encounter with the whale, the giant cetacean had bitten off one of his legs.

Melville, in writing about the whiteness of some wild creatures, mentioned the polar bear. "With reference to the polar bear," wrote Melville, "the irresponsible hideousness of the creature stands invested in the fleece of celestial innocence and love; and, hence, by bringing together two such opposite emotions in our minds, the polar bear frightens us with so unnatural a contrast. But even assuming all of this to be true; yet, were it not for the whiteness, you would not have that intensified terror."

What Melville meant by this statement was that the polar bear's white color was deceiving. Its white pelage, which he said symbolized innocence and love, was in marked contrast to the ferocious nature of the animal. Melville felt that the bear's whiteness added to the fear or terror which an encounter with the beast aroused in human beings.

But the whiteness of the polar bear, whatever emotions it may evoke, does not deter hunters from going out to meet the animal in battle. Among the Eskimos, a victory over a white bear elevates the hunter to a high position in the eyes of his peers. Even Eskimo boys dream of the day when they will meet and kill their first polar bear.

An Eskimo man and young boy, accompanied by several husky dogs, stare at a big polar bear on an ice ledge. The bear can go no further. It is trapped against a wall of ice. Facing its attackers with snarls of rage, the bear stands still, balancing itself on the precarious ledge.

Now the Eskimos and their fierce dogs close in on the bear. The man signals to the boy and the youth raises his harpoon, waiting for a chance to hurl it into the bear's body. The bear shifts on its feet like a wrestler waiting to grapple with an opponent.

One dog, more daring than the others, charges at the bear, hackles raised and teeth bared. But the bear is ready and merely swats the dog aside with a big paw. The dog tumbles and slides along the ice, yelping in pain.

Another dog rushes at the bear and is followed by the other. The bear is beset on both flanks. He strikes right and left with his huge paws and slashes at the dogs with his great teeth. Bits of dog hair and bear fur fly through the air as the fight reaches a furious peak.

Now the Eskimo man calls off the dogs. Tense and excited from the battle, the bear watches the man and boy with wary eyes. A nod from the man and the boy's harpoon sails through the air and pierces the bear's chest.

Roaring with pain, the great bear rears up and flails the air with his paws. He vainly tries to push the harpoon out of his chest. Now another harpoon stabs into his body. His movements become slower, and the snow turns red with his blood.

Gradually, the white bear sinks down on the ledge, eyes glazing with approaching death. He makes one last supreme effort to rise and then drops back on the ice. A loud roar turns into a sigh and in a few minutes, the great white bear is dead. The Eskimo man turns and pats the boy on the head, while the dogs sniff the dead bear.

In recent years, the legal hunting of polar bears has been controlled and reduced in most of the regions in which these bears are found. The Soviet Union has extended protection to polar bears within its land and water territories since 1960. Canada also affords some protection to the bears; no civilian of any Canadian province may kill a white bear. Eskimos in the Northwest Territory, however, may take two bears a year for food, clothing, and income.

Norway protects polar bears within its territorial waters and on its landmasses. Alaska, where polar bears have been hunted by sportsmen in small airplanes and helicopters as recently as a few years ago, now limits the hunting of these mammals—the state bans the hunting of the bears from aircraft.

In spite of a certain amount of protection, the polar bear populations are declining each year. Nobody knows exactly how many of the white bears live in the Arctic wastelands and on the ice packs. An accurate census is difficult to make in a range estimated to be more than five million square miles. Therefore, reports on polar bear numbers are often conflicting; some state the bears are declining in certain regions, others claim the bears are in abundant supply. The main reason for the contrasting reports is that the bears are constantly roaming from region to region, dropping their numbers in one region and raising them in another.

Polar bear conservation and management programs are hampered by the lack of accurate statistics on the populations. In the Canadian Archipelago, Hudson's

Bay, the Russian-owned Wrangell Islands, Novaya Zemlya, and Franz Josef Land, and the northern tip of Spitzbergen, protecting and managing the bears are made difficult by the movements of the mammals. Many of them roam away from protected areas and enter remote regions where they are exposed to pelagic hunting and other hazards.

It is quite clear that the conservation and management of the polar bears, whatever their true numbers may be, are international problems. An important keystone in any polar bear conservation program is the question of immediate jurisdiction over the bears. That is, the nation whose territories—land and water—the bears may occupy at any given time should assume responsibility for protecting them.

The problem of the polar bears has been the subject of a number of national and international meetings or conventions. One convention, which convened in Oslo, Norway, in 1973, had on its agenda the matter of polar bear populations. What the delegates wanted to know was just how many polar bears live in the Arctic and where are they more or less centered?

Estimates of the bear population (that is, the total population of all polar bears in all Arctic regions) ranged from 10,000 to 20,000, with most of the delegates agreeing that 20,000 was perhaps the correct estimate. Of this number, more than half lived and roamed across Arctic wastelands and ice packs in Canadian territories.

As for polar bears in United States territories, the majority of them live on ice packs or enter the territory, island and mainland, of Alaska. Denmark's polar bears are confined to the ice packs and coastal landmasses of Greenland. Norway's white bears are limited to that nation's Svalbard Archipelago in the Greenland Sea. Those polar bears in Soviet territories are found on Franz Josef Land, Novaya Zemyla, North Land, the New Siberian Islands, and Wrangell Island.

Most of the regions in which the polar bears are found are bleak and desolate. Hunters can operate in them with little fear of detection or apprehension. The patrolling of polar bear habitats is an extremely difficult operation, as difficult as that of policing the vast whaling regions of the sea. No nation has been able to stop the illegal killing of polar bears, mainly because it cannot provide the manpower and equipment necessary to follow and protect them.

An important factor in any conservation of wildlife is a knowledge of a particular animal's life cycle, habits, behavior, and population dynamics. Scientists are trying to learn more about the polar bears, especially their breeding capacities. It is known that the bears breed every other year and begin mating when they are from two and one-half to four years of age. Reproduction in captive polar bears, however, is a rare event, and there have been only a relatively few births of cubs in the various zoos of the world.

Any interference with the reproductive rate can adversely affect their populations. When one considers the late age at which the white bears breed and their alternate-year mating pattern, it is not difficult to imagine what might happen to their numbers if too many bears of breeding age are killed.

Scientists are also studying the migratory habits of the polar bears. Thousands of the white bears have been marked with paint, ear tags, and tattoos in an attempt to trace their wanderings. Canadian wildlife biologists have been especially active in this kind of research. Biologists in helicopters spend hours searching for polar bears in the remote regions of the Canadian Archipelago.

When polar bear tracks or slides (the slides are ruts or gouges in the snow made by bears sliding down slopes to reach lower levels of the terrain) are discovered by the airborne scientists, they are followed until they lead to a bear or group of bears. When a bear is located, a biologist shoots a tranquilizer dart into the bear's body. After the tranquilizer has taken effect, the biologist then goes to work. First, an ear tag is placed on the bear. Next, the bear is measured for length and a small premolar tooth extracted from the lower jaw. Later, this tooth will be examined as a means of determining the bear's age.

The ultimate aim of this and other polar bear research projects is to collect data that will help wildlife specialists to protect and manage the bears. Scientists hope that when enough data is in, it will enable them to prevent the bears from becoming rare or even extinct mammals.

Since the hunting of polar bears is now controlled over most of their range, one might ask just what is the problem now. Are the white bears declining in numbers? If so, why? There seems to be a general agreement that polar bears are declining in numbers. And there may be more than one reason for the reduced populations.

One reason is hunting. As noted, laws and conservation measures in themselves cannot stop poachers or illegal hunters from killing the bears. Also, while five nations—Canada, Denmark, Norway, the Soviet Union, and the United States—are signatories to treaties to protect the bears, other nations are not. Fishermen, sealers, and whalers from a number of nations are now entering Arctic waters to take fish, seals, and whales. A polar bear on an ice pack is, as it was in Admiral Peary's day, an alluring target, and many icebound bears are killed each year by sailors and fishermen.

The custom of allowing Eskimos and other natives to take a certain number of polar bears for oil, food, and clothing is a necessary and humane measure. But what about allowing them to take white bears for income, as in the case of Canadian Eskimos? This means that they can sell polar bear skins. Considering the high price of a polar bear skin today (perhaps several hundred dollars), some natives might be tempted to kill more than the alloted quota. Perhaps this factor needs reevaluation or at least close supervision, particularly when the true inventory of this natural resource is an unknown quantity.

Another reason for the decline in the polar bear numbers is alterations in their habitats and encroachment on their denning and feeding grounds by man. More and more incursions into Arctic regions are being made in the search for oil and minerals. The danger to the polar bears lies not so much in drilling or mining operations as in the sequel to these activities—the settlements, roads, cars, trucks, mills, and people that usually follow. These pose serious problems for the white bears.

Increased fishing and whaling activities in Arctic waters must also be regarded as a threat to the polar bears. Again, Japanese and Russian fishing trawlers and whaling ships are operating in the Arctic seas on a large scale. Polar bears, like the sea otters, now face strong competition for marine food supplies.

If the polar bear's primary food, fish and seals, is greatly reduced by fishing and sealing fleets, the bears may be forced to turn to other sources of food. They may increase their predation on musk oxen and reindeer, using these mammals as substitutes or what wildlife specialists call buffer species. When they do so, they will arouse the enmity of Eskimos and other people who raise reindeer and musk oxen herds, thus exposing themselves to elimination.

This kind of situation arose on the Great Plains in the nineteenth century. The plains grizzly bears preyed primarily on the bison. When the bison numbers were drastically reduced by contract hunters hired by ranchers and the railroads, the plains grizzlies were forced to turn to secondary species for food. These happened to be cattle, horses, and sheep. Again free-lance hunters were hired, and the plains grizzlies were soon eliminated for all time.

Oilspills in Arctic waters also constitute a threat to the polar bears since various members of the marine food chain are affected by the oil. A single major oilspill could seriously threaten the survival of the bears. Added to the hazard of oilspills is pollution from chemicals and pesticides. One dangerous chemical previously mentioned is PCB. This chemical, according to scientists, has the capability of damaging embryos and chromosomes. PCB has already been found in the systems of a number of polar bears.

The conservation and management of the polar bears offer us a unique opportunity to apply new knowledge and technology to save a valuable natural resource. We also have a chance to avoid the mistakes of the past, which included a wanton waste of wildlife. There is, besides, a challenge to all nations: join together in a cooperative international program to save the polar bears and other endangered marine life.

We cannot forget that the loss of a marine mammal is a world loss. Now that the Arctic regions are being invaded by man, we must not permit the destruction of the polar bears simply because they—like other wildlife before them—are in the way of progress.

·12·

Birds of the Sea and Shore

June, 1844. Eldey Island off the southwestern coast of Iceland. Two hunters, Jon Brandsson and Sigourour Isleffson, pick their way over rocks and pebbles. Many birds fly up in alarm, filling the air with indignant cries at the intrusion into their nesting grounds.

The two hunters ignore the birds flying about them. They continue along the shore, scanning the rocks and declivities. They seek a special bird.

They move on, pausing now and then to examine abandoned nests. Then, just ahead, near a large rock, stand two odd-looking birds, their beady eyes on the hunters.

Quickly, the hunters stride toward the birds, raising their heavy clubs. The birds do not take flight but remain watching the men coming toward them. Then, with rapid motions, the men rush at the birds, swinging the clubs.

Well-aimed blows instantly kill the birds. The two hunters are exuberant, for they have killed two birds that have been scarce for a long time.

What the hunters do not know is that these two birds are all that is left of a dying species. They are the last specimens of the Great Auk, a once populous species that ranged over a wide area of the North Atlantic coasts.

With their clubs, Brandsson and Isleffson have catapulted the Great Auk into extinction. The species is no more. It is consigned to oblivion. Nothing that man can do—now or in the future—will ever bring back the Great Auk.

The Great Auk, of course, is gone—wiped out by overhunting in a relatively short time. Thousands of other birds were hunted for their meat and plumage, and their nests robbed of eggs. The nineteenth century was truly the Dark Ages for all kinds of wildlife. Ducks, brant, gulls, terns, lesser auks, albatrosses, curlews, godwits, phalaropes, dowitchers, murres, kittiwakes, skimmers, guillemots, skuas, jaegers, and penguins lived in the sea and along the shores. Estuaries and marshes contained the ibises, cranes, soras, and pelicans. Into these sea and coastal areas went hordes of hunters, killing birds and stealing eggs.

By the end of the nineteenth century, many of the sea and shore bird populations were greatly reduced. Even the ubiquitous sea gulls, the noisy birds of the sea and shore, were suffering severe drops in numbers as plume hunters invaded the beaches and coastal zones. Only by the enactment of some hunting laws and protective measures were the birds spared the fate of the Great Auk, passenger pigeon, and Carolina parakeet. When the fad for plumed hats faded away and plume hunters no longer were out in force, the sea and shore birds—at least the majority of species—had a respite from exploitation. But many years were required before some sorely depleted species were able to rebuild their numbers.

Today, although some hunting still goes on, the sea and shore birds face new hazards. Alterations in their habitats, competition with man for the marine food supplies, and pollution now threaten the lives and populations of these birds. Each of these hazards takes a high toll of sea and shore birdlife.

Alterations of seabird habitats is unquestionably a major threat to a number of species. So is the encroachment on or takeover of nesting sites on oceanic islands. The situation of the Laysan albatrosses *(Diomedea immutabilis)* is a prime example of this kind of hazard. Laysan albatrosses, or gooneybirds, as sailors call them, have been persecuted for more than a quarter of a century on their nesting grounds on various Pacific islands. Pacific islands under the jurisdiction of the United States are used as air bases and communication centers. The problem, according to the Navy, is that the gooneybirds are in the way; more than that, they are dangerous to planes and personnel, for the goonies congregate on runways and endanger the takeoff and landing of planes.

The Navy has spent considerable time, money, and manpower in trying to get rid of the gooneybirds. Naval authorities claim the birds are trespassers, unwanted

LAYSAN ALBATROSS

birds. If the situation is regarded in its true scientific light, it is the Navy, and not the gooneybirds, that is trespassing on the islands. These islands have been the nesting grounds for the albatrosses for hundreds, possibly thousands of years. And the problem now is simply one of man and birds competing for the same habitat.

Albatrosses are magnificent seabirds that spend part of their lives on islands, when they are mating and nesting, and part flying over a great expanse of the sea north of the equator. The big birds are awe-inspiring, with their large wings and white plumage. Albatrosses were once regarded by mariners with superstition.

Turning again to Melville's *Moby Dick*, a repository of information about sea creatures as well as an epic sea story, there is this passage about the albatross:

> "I remember the first albatross I ever saw. It was during a prolonged gale in waters hard upon the Antarctic seas. From my forenoon watch below, I ascended the overclouded deck; and there, dashed upon the main hatches, I saw a regal, feathery thing of unspotted whiteness, and with a hooked Roman bill sublime. At intervals, it arched forth its vast archangel wings as if to embrace some holy ark.
>
> Wondrous flutterings and throbbings shook it. Though bodily unharmed, it uttered cries, as some king's ghost in supernatural distress. Through its inexpressible, strange eyes, methought I peeped into the secrets which took hold of God."

While Melville's description of the albatross may be attacked as wholly unscientific, it is, nevertheless, a fitting account of the emotional feelings an albatross can evoke from an observer seeing this spectacular bird for the first time.

The awe and superstition that the albatross is supposed to have aroused in sailors were emphasized in Samuel Taylor Coleridge's famous narrative poem, *The Rime of the Ancient Mariner*. Coleridge's ancient mariner, it will be recalled, killed an albatross, a bird that sailors believed brought the vital sea breezes necessary to sail the ships.

Even the ancient mariner realized that he had committed a vile act by killing the albatross:

> *"And I had done a hellish thing,*
> *And it would work'em woe:*
> *For all averr'd I had killed the bird*
> *That made the breeze to blow.*
> *Ah, wretch! said they, the bird to slay*
> *That made the breeze to blow!"*

Yet, the story of the ancient mariner to the contrary, most of the awe and superstition surrounding albatrosses was simply legend. Thousands of these sea birds were killed by the very mariners to whom the bird was supposed to be sacred.

In reality, albatrosses were just another form of sea life to be killed for one purpose or other. Some mariners killed albatrosses for the meat, although, judging from all accounts, the meat was very tough. When the British navigator, Sir Francis Drake, sailed his ships on a circumnavigational tour of the world in 1577–79, members of his crew killed many albatrosses for food. Also, Captain Cook mentions in his writings that his sailors shot albatrosses for the ship tables.

But albatrosses were killed not only for their meat but for sport. Sailors becalmed in lonely waters, such as the Sargasso Sea, often whiled away the time by catching albatrosses on fishing lines and hooks baited with salt pork. The albatrosses dived at the bits of pork and became snared on the sharp hooks. Hundreds of albatrosses were taken in this manner. William Scoresby, explorer and navigator, mentioned that in 1856, albatross killing was a widespread sport among the crews of ships that sailed to Australia.

However, albatrosses shot or hooked by sailors were not wasted. Their alabaster white feathers were prizes to take home to wives and girl friends. Whole skins of the birds were turned into feather rugs. Even the feet of the albatrosses were utilized; sailors converted the webbing of the feet into tobacco pouches. The slight oiliness of the skin helped to keep tobacco from drying out.

To return to the gooneybirds on the Pacific islands: the war between the goonies and the American Navy still continues. Thousands of these albatrosses have been destroyed. Conservationists and humanitarians have protested the slaughter of the goonies, especially the methods employed to eliminate the birds. The Navy has countered with the argument that it must eliminate or at least reduce the number of gooneybirds on the islands because they endanger the lives of Navy personnel and cause costly damage to planes and other equipment on the islands.

Far to the south in Antarctic waters and on the fringes of South America and nearby islands, another bird is troubled by man and his activities. This is the penguin, the bird that wears a tuxedolike plumage and walks upright. There are seventeen species of penguins distributed in the colder regions of the South Pacific and South Atlantic Oceans.

Life is naturally harsh for the penguins. Their nesting grounds are crowded, and the birds must contend with predators from the sea and air. Skuas, a predatory gull-like bird, kill baby penguins. Sharks snatch up penguins swimming in the sea. But, again, these are natural hazards and nature tries to compensate for them. Man's hunting of penguins and penguin eggs and his encroachment on their habitats add to the burdens of these unique birds.

Penguins belong to the order *Sphenisciformes* and are the most completely marine in habits of all the seabirds. They have webbed toes and wings modified into flippers that cannot be folded back like the wings of other birds. These modifications make the penguins highly adapted to their rugged environment. In the sea, penguins can swim as fast as a seal. On land, they are bipedal, walking awkwardly but rapidly in an upright position. When in a hurry to reach the sea, penguins will often slide along the ground. Penguins are gregarious birds and live in large colonies that remind one of crowded cities.

One species of penguin under heavy pressures from man's hunting and land development activities is the gentoo *(Pygoscelis papua)* of the Falkland Islands. The gentoo penguins are about two feet long; they are extremely fast swimmers and feed on krill and squid. Gentoos have white bands across their faces, stretching from eye to eye.

Gentoos and other penguins have been hunted in the Falkland Island region ever since the islands were first settled by the French in 1764. A Frenchman, Louis de Bougainville, led a number of settlers to the remote Falkland Islands. Ever since the time of de Bougainville, wildlife on the islands and in the nearby waters has been

GENTOO PENGUIN

heavily exploited. In addition to hunting, penguins and other birds were subjected to losses of habitats and food. Large areas of wildlife habitat were destroyed by the introduction of cattle and sheep to the islands. Soil erosion, a result of overgrazing by livestock, proved damaging to vegetation upon which birds and other wildlife depended for food and shelter. Tussock grass, for instance, was an important plant for many birds and it, too, was destroyed by the alterations on the islands.

For more than two centuries, there has been a heavy harvest of penguins in the Falkland Island areas. In the early days of the island settlements, sailors and colonists relished the flesh of the birds and the taste of penguin eggs. The eggs were gathered by the thousands and preserved in seal oil contained in wooden kegs. Later, when sealing around the Falklands dropped off because of the sharp decline in seals, hunters turned to the gentoo penguins as an alternate source of oil. Consequently, gentoos and other penguins were trapped, netted, clubbed, and shot for their valuable oil.

In a two-year period (1864–66), seven ships rendered more than 60,000 gallons of pure penguin oil from birds taken in the area of Fort Stanley, the capital of the Falkland Islands. Penguin rookeries on other islands were quickly depleted of their birds and eggs. Over a half-million penguins were slaughtered for their oil. Entire populations were wiped out on some of the islands; with no young or chicks to replace the heavy losses among the adults, the penguin populations went into a steep decline. Some species, notably the macaroni penguin *(Eudypte chrysolophus)* and the king penguin *(Aptenodytes patagonia)*, became exceedingly rare as a result of the penguin pogroms. The king penguin is the second largest species after the emperor penguin *(Aptenodytes forsteri)*, which also suffered heavy losses.

Penguins are still hunted today. Although the birds are protected in many regions, enforcement of conservation and hunting laws is difficult because of the vast territory to be policed. Poachers kill hundreds of penguins and in some regions, permits are issued for the taking of penguin eggs. Penguin-egg collecting amounts to about 40,000 eggs a year.

The total population of all seventeen species of penguins is unknown at the present time. Even the number of individual species is nothing more than a rough estimate. Reports on penguin populations, like those of polar bears, are conflicting. Documentary films showing swarms or colonies of penguins mating and nesting on barren landmasses are misleading, for they depict only selected colonies and habitats. The vital question now is that while the penguins seem to be maintaining safe numbers, how long will this situation last in view of the increased use and disturbance of the sea and its natural resources?

Sea and shore birds, because of their marine food chains, are exceptionally vulnerable to pollution. Terns, gull-like birds, have been adversely affected by the ingestion of chemicals by way of their particular food chain. A three-year study of terns in eastern Long Island Sound revealed some marked changes in the birds as a result of chemical pollution. Thirty-nine abnormal tern chicks were discovered in one colony. The chicks were deformed in a number of ways; for example, some had crossed beaks, an eye missing, no feathers, misformed feet, and swollen bodies.

Researchers found high levels of PCBs in the tissues of chicks and adult terns. PCBs were also discovered in fish eaten by the terns. The PCBs have chemical properties similar to those of DDT and tend to concentrate in the fatty tissues of birds and mammals.

Long Island Sound, along with the Baltic Sea, the Mediterranean Sea, and the coastal waters of California, has the distinction of being one of the most highly polluted marine areas in the world. What has happened to the terns in Long Island Sound holds a special warning: if PCBs cause abnormalities among terns and other seabirds, think what may happen to human beings who eat fish contaminated with PCBs. One very real possibility is birth deformities.

Chemical and pesticide pollution has seriously affected the populations of the brown pelicans *(Pelicanus occidentalis)*, the birds with the suitcaselike bills that live in the coastal regions of the southern United States and the California coastal waters. The numbers of brown pelicans have declined in these regions, and the Louisiana colonies were wiped out as a result of chemical and pesticide pollution. In 1972, the Environmental Protection Agency banned the use of DDT, but other chemicals and pesticides continued to flow into the coastal waters inhabited by the eastern brown pelicans. The loss of the brown pelicans in Louisiana waters was all the more deplorable since the pelican was the official state bird of Louisiana. To help Louisiana restore brown pelicans in its territorial waters, the state of Florida donated about 200 pelicans as foundation stock for Barataria Bay, some seventy miles south of New Orleans, where the brown pelicans were completely eradicated in the early 1960s.

The brown pelican colonies are also being threatened by the encroachment of man and his activities. Nesting sites of this fish-eating bird are invaded by people. Many of the nesting birds are frightened by the invasions of their sites. A most damaging result is that many pelican eggs are addled because the birds abandon their clutch of eggs. Also, many eggs are stolen from pelican nests by vandals and other wildlife looters.

Ornithologist Ralph Schrieber of Seabirds Research, Inc., has found that pelicans are exposed to a new danger. The plastic rings or holders of the common six-pack beer or soda cans are tossed into the water by fishermen, hunters, and boaters. These plastic rings become death traps for pelicans. Fish will nibble at the rings. Then the brown pelicans go after the fish and some of them poke their bills through one of the plastic rings. In too many cases, according to Schrieber, the pelicans cannot get the plastic ring off their bills. The plastics will not rot away, and, since the birds cannot open their bills, they starve to death.

Another threat to the brown pelicans is that of being caught on fishermen's hooks or entangled in fishing lines. Schrieber estimates that more than eighty percent of the pelicans handled by him in the past few years have had hooks or lines attached to them. He also discovered more than one hundred dead pelicans in mangrove trees, snagged there by monofilament fishing lines.

Elsewhere in the world's seas and coastal waters, other birds are experiencing difficulties from chemical and pesticide pollution, oilspills, loss of habitats, danger from human activities, and competition with man for the food of the sea. Oceanic and shore birds are in just as much need of protection and management as fish, shellfish, marine mammals, and sea turtles.

What happens to the sea and shore birds in the years ahead is of importance, for they, too, are interwoven into the web of life and have a role to play in the ecology of the sea. And at the least, their welfare should be incorporated into any law of the sea that the nations of the world must eventually draft and enact.

·13·

Return to the Sea

The call of the sea is stronger now than ever before. Man looks hopefully to the great ocean environment and its natural resources to cure some of *his* troubles. A ravaged land environment, an ever-increasing human population with huge demands for food, a diminishing supply of energy fuels on land, a need for more chemicals and minerals, and a general improvement in transportation: these are the major human problems that the sea is expected to ease in the years ahead.

Is the sea capable of curing or easing these human difficulties? Can it provide a continuous supply of protein foods? The answer is a qualified yes. Acre for acre, the sea's fertility is equal to that of unspoiled farmland. Yet only about three percent of the world's food comes from the sea. More than seventy-five percent of the world's population now receives insufficient protein, and about sixty-five percent is close to protein starvation. Protein deficiencies impair both the mental and physical development of children, even in the United States, the so-called land of plenty.

The irony is that the sea abounds in protein foods. However, we are not efficiently utilizing this great storehouse of food. Only a few nations have technically advanced fishery industries. Others, including the United States, India, and developing countries along the African coasts, need to upgrade their fishing fleets and operations.

On a world basis, the fishery industry—in contrast to other methods of obtaining food (for example, agriculture)—is still very primitive. It is comparable to the hunting and food-gathering efforts of Neolithic people eight or nine thousand years ago.

Unquestionably, the evolution and development of agriculture, with its crop production and livestock raising, revolutionized man's food procurement capabilities. When man became a farmer, he became less dependent upon the uncertain fruits of the hunt. Yet when man turned to the sea as a source of food, he never properly farmed or managed the ocean's natural resources. Man has not tilled the sea for food, he has merely plundered it.

As the world's population grows, more nations are looking to the sea to help them solve their food problems. Each year, there is a steady increase in the number of trawlers off the continental coasts. The intense search for fish and shellfish creates conflicts between nations. Mismanagement of fish and shellfish stocks, now and in the past, has reduced the supply. Furthermore, the big question of territorial waters has not been settled, even though the representatives of 150 nations met in the first conference on the law of the sea in Caracas, Venezuela, in the summer of 1974.

The question of territorial waters is a crucial one, not only in regard to fish and shellfish stocks, but also for the control of pollution. Many countries have some coastal waters, even if limited. The jurisdiction over these waters extends over but a relatively small portion of the sea. What lies beyond a nation's territorial waters is the open sea or international waters. For centuries, the open sea has belonged to all nations. Fishermen, sealers, and whalers from many nations entered the open waters and took fish, shellfish, seals, and whales with impunity. As long as the ships of one nation did not infringe on the territorial waters of another, nobody cared what happened to the open sea environment.

Now the situation has changed. We must protect both territorial and international waters from overexploitation of natural resources and the dangers of pollution. The knowledge being accumulated from various oceanographic research projects, such as the United Nations Food and Agriculture Organization's survey of potential seafood regions of the sea and the United States' International Decade of Ocean Exploration, should be made available to all nations. Equally important, this knowledge must be applied by nations, individually in the case of territorial waters, and collectively in the case of the open sea or international waters.

In recent years, we have read and heard much about mariculture or sea farming as a means of obtaining more food from the sea. In some quarters, mariculture has been touted as the main method of obtaining food in the future. Mariculture is feasible and is being conducted in a number of sea areas. But it is not being conducted on any large commercial scale. There are many obstacles in the way, and sea farming is not as easy or simple as some reports would have one believe.

First of all, there is the condition of the sea itself. The sea is in a state of constant motion and change. Therefore, it does not always present a stable or uniform set of growing conditions, except perhaps in sheltered bays and estuaries. A wheatfield, orchard, berry patch, vegetable garden, or beef cattle feedlot remains fairly constant as a food-producing region in contrast to the sometimes violent changes that occur in many marine areas. Thus, mariculture can be carried out only in selected regions of the sea that provide the proper growing conditions and are free from pollution.

Another consideration in any large-scale mariculture is the availability of nutrients. Ninety percent of the sea's nutrients are trapped beyond the continental shelves. They are out in the deeps where they are not readily available to marine life, most of which breed and grow in the bays, estuaries, and shallow coastal waters. Sunlight, a vital component of any kind of farming, is absent in the deeps. Only when nutrients in the deeps are carried toward the surface by the upwelling of water do diatoms and other phytoplankton bloom and prosper.

Then what about applying fertilizers or other nutrients to sea areas for the purpose of increasing the yields of seafood? This can be done—and is being done—but not on a large scale. The application of fertilizers or plant and animal foods to large sea farming areas is simply not economically feasible at this time.

It has also been suggested that we utilize plankton as human food. Again, there are some obstacles to such a practice. One is that the harvesting of plankton—at least with present equipment and methods—is too costly. Also, some plankton are poisonous, and great care must be exercised to cull out these dangerous members of the marine food chain.

All of this is not to say that phytoplankton and zooplankton will not be used as human food some day. Some nations have already started programs to ascertain which plankton can be used for human food and how they can be farmed or managed. For example, Japanese scientists, under pressure to cease whaling, are studying plankton as a future source of protein food. The particular plankton under study are small, shrimplike animals known as krill. Krill often reach an overall length of two inches and are the primary food of the baleen or *Mysticeti* whales.

There are abundant supplies of krill in Antarctic waters. These sea animals are rich in tryptophan, an important amino acid that forms a major protein nutrient. Krill are also a source of vitamins and calcium. Yet, the main problem, as in other mariculture projects, is to find a commercially workable way of harvesting this kind of plankton. The harvesting of krill for a mass market is out of the question now.

Thus, we not only need to learn more about plankton and other living resources of the sea, with the ultimate aim of using them as food, but we must find economical ways of harvesting them. Perhaps, for the time being, it might be wiser to let the fish, marine mammals, and other potential seafood animals in the sea eat the plankton. Our efforts should be focused on the conservation and wise management of all of the sea's living resources: fish, shellfish, porpoises, whales, seals, sea otters, birds, turtles, and polar bears.

Our increased use of the sea goes beyond the need to find more food. Land supplies of fossil fuels and important minerals are dwindling each year as domestic and industrial use gobbles them up. We are in the midst of a severe energy crisis. Mineral-poor nations must find new sources of these natural resources, especially when some nations rich in fossil fuels and minerals now employ them as political levers. Consequently, exploration of the seabeds for fossil fuels, particularly oil, is now the major concern of many nations.

Exploration for and development of the sea's oil deposits are costly ventures. The discovery of oil is based on a knowledge of the origin of this valuable substance, the structure of the earth, the physical properties of sediments deposited in different regions, and the hydrodynamics of ground water flow. What all of this means is that locating oil—in the sea and on land—is not simply a matter of sailing or walking over an area with a dowsing wand. It means that extensive research, exploration, and drilling, all at a great cost, must be carried out.

Oil experts claim that tapping offshore oil reserves is the keystone for building up domestic petroleum reserves. They state that the fears of environmentalists, namely, that oil drilling operations will disturb and pollute the ocean environment, are without any basis. Oilmen point out that in the twenty-five years of offshore drilling, there have been only four accidents. Of these four, only one—the spill off the coast of Santa Barbara, California —caused any extensive contamination of shore areas and destruction of wildlife.

Perhaps four accidents in oil drilling operations in the sea is a fair record of performance, considering the hundreds of oil rigs in use. But what about the future? More and more oil rigs are rising up from the sea, near shore and far out over the continental shelves. As the sea becomes dotted with more oil rigs the chances of accidents will increase. There may well be more than four major oilspills.

Most people understand the need to find more fuel for energy. They also understand that the sea must be tapped for its oil. What they do not understand—or condone—is the tendency of oil companies to explore and drill for oil without regard for the impact on the ocean environment. To many conservationists and environmental protectionists, the attitude of the oil companies, as well as mining interests, is reminiscent of that displayed in the nineteenth century by exploiters of natural resources. At that time, land developers and natural resource exploiters simply went ahead with their operations with a total disregard for the impact on the environment. The federal government, state and territorial governments not only permitted the overexploitation of minerals and the destruction of wildlife, but assisted the exploiters with land grants, tax benefits, and favorable legislation.

If the ocean environment is to receive even a moderate amount of protection, all drilling operations must be closely monitored. Industry will always do things the cheapest way, even if it means the destruction of something. Therefore, the responsibility of protecting the marine environment cannot be left entirely to the oil companies or mining interests. Certainly a national or state government should not relinquish control of offshore and continental shelf drilling or mining operations to the oil and mining interests. Both the federal government and state governments—as stewards of natural resources that belong to all the people—must be given the power to halt hazardous or questionable drilling or mining operations in territorial waters. Furthermore, that power must be exercised to remove any threat to the ocean environment.

While drilling for oil in the sea is a reality, mining the seabed for minerals is just leaving the research stage. Mining companies in the United States, Japan, West Germany, France, and the Soviet Union have already explored the seabed and assayed many of its minerals. The explorations and their findings promise a massive rush by nations to take minerals from the sea.

One American company has built a huge mining ship, the *Glomar Explorer*. This ship is capable of scooping up minerals and metals from the seabed at a prodigious rate. It weighs 35,000 tons, has a length of 618 feet, and a width, or beam, of 115 feet. The *Glomar Explorer* carries a crew of more than a hundred seamen and technicians and is indeed a floating mechanical giant that has the potential for disturbing and possibly destroying vast regions of the ocean environment.

There are a number of considerations in the mining of the ocean floor. For one, the impact of deep-sea mining operations on the delicate marine ecosystems, particularly fishery resources, is not presently known. Also, will there be a conflict of interests; that is, will oil drilling and mining operations take precedence over the harvesting of

GLOMAR EXPLORER

seafood? It is a possibility, considering the power and influence of oil and mining industries and the relative weakness of fishing industries.

Another important sea-mining consideration is that developed nations have an unfair advantage over undeveloped nations. Some undeveloped nations have coastal waters but little or no technical knowledge or sea-mining equipment. Custom has always dictated that international waters belong to all nations, and it should remain so. No single nation, or coalition of nations, should be allowed to exploit the sea's resources, living and mineral, to the exclusion of another nation.

At the opening of the United Nations Conference on the Law of the Sea in Venezuela in the summer of 1974, President Carlos Andres Perez of Venezuela told the delegates of 150 nations that "The sea must serve a humane policy of distribution of wealth and of natural resources for all men, and not for a devious accumulation of self-serving nations, consortiums, or owners of technology."

Certainly any new code of international laws for the use of the sea and its natural resources must include President Perez' credo. But it must go beyond just sharing the wealth of the sea among all nations. Any code of laws for the use of the sea must contain strong provisions for protecting and wisely managing the sea and its resources; otherwise there will be no wealth to share.

The new law of the sea, when and if it ever materializes, must contain mandatory regulations to ensure continuing stocks of fish, shellfish, dugongs, manatees, seals, sea otters, porpoises, whales, sea turtles, sea and shore birds, and polar bears. Furthermore, there must be a means to enforce any and all regulations geared to protect the sea's natural resources. Those commercial interests, shipping lines, industries, mining companies, and others that flout or ignore the sea law and continue to plunder and pollute the ocean environment must be regarded as pirates—robbers and looters of the sea—and treated accordingly.

Only a code of sea laws, respected and obeyed by all nations, can halt the degradation of the sea and destruction of its living resources. All nations, including the forty-one African nations that did not send delegates to the 1974 Conference on the Law of the Sea, must join together to protect the sea. There is no place for isolation. Even landlocked nations, such as Switzerland and Bolivia, have a stake in the sea's future. All nations engage in some form of trade with other nations. Each relies on other nations for vital materials and supplies, many of which come from the sea.

Although the results of the 1974 Law of the Sea Conference were disappointing in that the delegates did not produce a set of laws for the use and management of the sea, the fact that 150 nations did send delegates to discuss the problems of the sea is significant. It means that these nations realize that the ultimate fate of the sea and the welfare of its natural resources lie in the hands of all nations.

Another conference was scheduled to convene in

Geneva during March, 1975. Unfortunately, even if the delegates can work out some of the major problems which developed during the 1974 conference, any decisions made at Geneva will not be implemented for some time to come. In the meantime, the ocean environment remains exposed to pollution and human predation. In the absence of a code of laws for the sea, concerned nations must act as watchdogs of the sea, taking whatever steps are necessary to protect the great ocean environment and its natural resources.

Above all, nations and their peoples must not yield to commercial or industrial interests that would exploit the sea at any costs. Nor should Americans and other peoples allow the present food and energy shortages to serve as an excuse to ransack and loot the sea. All nations and all peoples should reject the arguments that say that if people want food and energy, then there must be a relaxation—or even a revocation—of environmental controls. Such arguments are misleading and deceptive, for we have enough knowledge and technology to use the sea and its resources without destroying them.

The vast and mysterious sea holds great promise as a treasure chest of natural resources and recreation for all humanity. But the sea can fulfill this promise only if it is protected and its resources wisely managed. To this end, the peoples of all nations must, like Prince Hamlet, "take arms against a sea of troubles, and by opposing, end them."

Suggested Reading

Bays and Estuaries
Duddleson, William, "The Miracle of Point Reyes," *Living Wilderness*, (Summer, 1971), pp. 15–24.
Johns, Will, *Estuaries—America's Most Vulnerable Frontiers*, Washington, D.C.: National Wildlife Federation, 1965.
Shepherd, Elizabeth, *Arms of the Sea*, New York: Lothrop, Lee & Shepard, 1973.

Exploration of the Sea
Cousteau, Jacques, *Window in the Sea*, New York: World Publications, 1973.
Pennington, Howard, *New Ocean Explorers*, Boston: Little, Brown, 1972.
Villiers, Alan, *Captain James Cook*, New York: Scribner, 1967.

Fiction and General Books about the Sea
Gordon, Bernard L., ed., *Man and the Sea*, New York: Natural History Press, 1972.
Graham, Frank, Jr., *Where the Place Called Morning Lies: A*

Personal View of the American Environment, New York: Viking Press, 1973.

Melville, Herman, *Moby Dick*, New York: Hendricks House, 1962.

Fish and Fishery Industries

Doliber, Earl, *Lobstering Inshore and Offshore*, Camden, Maine: International Marine Publications Co., 1973.

Jensen, Albert, *The Cod*, New York: Thomas Crowell, 1972.

Jones, Edward C., *Salmon Fishing in the Northwest*, Concord: Stonewall Press, 1973.

McClain, Pete, "Oystering Is a Way of Life," *New Jersey Outdoors*, Vol. 1 (May–June 1974), pp. 30–31.

Netboy, Anthony, *The Atlantic Salmon*, Boston: Houghton, Mifflin, 1968.

Shapiro, Sidney, ed., *Our Changing Fisheries*, Washington, D.C.: U.S. Government Printing Office, 1971.

Mariculture

Bardach, John E., John H. Ruther, and William O. McLarney, *Aquaculture: The Farming & Husbandry of Freshwater and Marine Organisms*, New York: John Wiley & Sons, 1972.

Cousteau, Jacques, *Quest for Food*, New York: World Publications, 1973.

Palmer, H. U. E., "Recycling Wastes for Mariculture," *Sea Frontiers*, Vol. 19 (November–December 1973), pp. 369–373.

Ocean Environment

Berrill, N. J., *The Life of the Ocean*, New York: McGraw-Hill, 1966.

Carson, Rachel, *The Sea Around Us*, New York: Signet, 1961.

National Oceanic and Atmospheric Administration, *The Marine Environment and Oceanic Life*, Washington, D.C.: U.S. Government Printing Office, 1973.

Smith, F. G. Walton, *The Seas in Motion*, New York: Thomas Crowell, 1973.

Oceanography

Daugherty, Charles M., *Searchers of the Sea: Pioneers in Oceanography*, New York: Viking Press, 1961.

Gross, M. Grant, *Oceanography: A View of the Earth*, Englewood Cliffs, Prentice-Hall, 1972.

Pennington, Howard, *The New Ocean Explorers*, Boston: Little, Brown, 1972.

Telfer, Dorothy, *Exploring the World of Oceanography*, Chicago: Children's Press, 1968.

Polar Bears

McCoy, J. J., "The Near-sighted Ones," *Wild Enemies*, New York: Hawthorn, 1974.

Perry, Richard, *World of the Polar Bear*, Seattle: University of Washington Press, 1966.

Rue, Leonard Lee, III, *Pictorial Guide to the Mammals of North America*, New York: Thomas Crowell, 1967.

Pollution

Marx, Wesley, *The Frail Ocean*, New York: Ballantine Books, 1970.

Ogren, Larry, and James Chess, "A Marine Kill on New Jersey Wrecks," *Underwater Naturalist*, (Fall, 1969), American Littoral Society.

Pearce, John B., "Biological Survey of Submerged Refuse," *Marine Pollution Bulletin*, Vol. 3 (October 1972), pp. 157–158.

Young, James S., and Charles I. Gibson, "Effect of Thermal Effluent on Migrating Menhaden," *Marine Pollution Bulletin*, (July 1972), pp. 94–95.

Porpoises

Alpers, Anthony, *Dolphins, the Myth and the Mammals*, Boston: Houghton Mifflin, 1961.

Morris, Kenneth S., *The Porpoise Watcher*, New York: W. W. Norton, 1974.

Wood, Forest G., *Marine Mammals and Man*, Washington-New York: Robert B. Luce, Inc., 1973.

Seabirds

Darwin, Charles, *Voyage of the Beagle*, New York: Bantam, 1972.

International Oceanographic Foundation, "Plight of the Pelicans," *Sea Secrets*, Vol. 18 (January–February 1974).

Saunders, David, *Seabirds*, New York: Grosset and Dunlop, 1973.

Vaucher, Charles, *Seabirds*, Philadelphia: Dufours edition, 1963.

Seals

Farre, Rowena, *Seal Morning*, New York: Ace Books, 1957.

Maxwell, Gavin, *Seals of the World*, Boston: Houghton, Mifflin, 1967.

Stuart, Frank S., *Seal's World*, New York: Pyramid Publications, 1972.

Sea Otters

McDearmon, Kay, *Day in the Life of a Sea Otter*, New York: Dodd, 1973.

Seed, Alice, *Sea Otter: In Eastern North Pacific Waters*, Seattle: Pacific Search, 1972.

United States Department of the Interior, *Seals, Sea Lions, and Sea Otters*, Washington, D. C.: U. S. Government Printing Office.

Sea Turtles

Bustard, Robert, *Sea Turtles*, New York: Taplinger Publications, 1973.

Carr, Archie, *So Excellent a Fishe*, New York: Natural History Press, 1967.

Jacobs, Francine, *Sea Turtles*, New York: William Morrow & Co., 1972.

Sirenians

Hartman, D. S., "Florida's Manatees: Mermaids in Peril," *National Geographic*, Vol. 136 (September 1969), pp. 342–353.

Hartman, J. E., "Manatee: Siren of the Sea," *National Wildlife*, Vol. 7 (October 1969), pp. 38–39.

Valentry, Duane, "Sea Cows That Would Not Breed," *Sea Frontiers*, Vol. 19 (September–October 1973), pp. 290–291.

Whales

Chatterton, E. K., *Whalers and Whaling*, Detroit: Gale, 1973.

Cousteau, Jacques, *Whale: Mighty Monarch of the Sea*, New York: Doubleday, 1972.

Olmstead, Francis, *Incidents of a Whaling Voyage*, New York: Dover, 1969.

Robertson, Robert, *Of Whales and Men*, Westminster, Maryland: Knopf, 1954.

Small, George L., *The Blue Whale*, New York: Columbia University Press, 1972.

Index

Alaska, 86, 103–10, 144
Albatrosses, 155–58
Antarctica, 96–97, 169
Arctic, the, 137–50
    oil spills in, 149–50
Audubon Society, National, 82, 135
Australia, 71, 116

Bacteria, 20–21, 33–34
Baltic Sea, 98, 162
Baronov, Alexander Andreyevich, 105–7
Bartram, William, 113–14
Bays and estuaries, 23–39
Benthic life, 16, 32
BHC, 19
Birds, 111, 151–64
    extinct, 151–52
    oilspill dangers to, 13–14

California, 101, 105, 108, 162, 171
Canada
    Atlantic salmon fishing and, 53
    fur sealing by, 88, 90, 91, 93, 94, 96
    polar bears of, 144, 147, 148
    whaling and, 71, 83
Caribbean Sea, 8, 128–31, 133, 135
Carr, Archie, 125, 129, 130, 134
Cholera, 20
Cousteau, James, 45, 120, 122

DDT, 6, 19, 111, 162
Denmark, 50–53, 148
Dolphins, 55–57
Dugongs, 114, 116–19, 123–24

Endangered Species Act (1969), 133
Enrichment, definition of, 15

Environmental Protection Agency (EPA), 19, 31, 37, 38, 162
Estuaries, 23–39
    definition of, 28
Euphotic zone, 28–29

Falkland Islands, 159–61
Fish, 16, 17, 23–27, 40–54, 166
    mass kills of, 29–30
    nuclear power plants and, 31
    species approach to harvesting of, 44–45
Florida, 122, 124, 130, 133, 163
Food and Agriculture Organization (FAO), 46, 167
Freon, 20
Fur seals, 85–99

Georges Bank, 43
Grand Banks, 29
Great Auk, 151–52
Great Britain, 40–41, 42, 71, 98
Greenland, 49–51, 98, 140, 146

Hackensack Meadowlands Commission, 34
Hanna, James, 104
Hawaii, 125–28, 130–31
Humane Society of the United States, 94–95

Iceland, 40–41, 42, 71, 151
International Commission for the Northwest Atlantic Fisheries (ICNAF), 51–52
International Convention on the Prevention of Marine Pollution, 38
International Whaling Commission (IWC), 74–76, 79, 81–82

Japan, 17, 20
    fishing by, 42, 43, 149

fur seals and, 90–91, 93
plankton studied by, 169
porpoises destroyed by, 58
sea otters and, 107
whaling by, 71, 75, 80–83, 149

Krill, 169

Law of the Sea Conference (1974),
    44–45, 166, 174–76
Lead, 18
Long Island waters, 13, 20–21,
    29–31, 36–37, 161–62

Manatees, 119–24
Mariculture (sea farming), 167–70
Marine Mammals Act of 1972,
    64–67
Marine Protection, Research, and
    Sanctuaries Act of 1972, 37–
    38
Mediterranean Sea, 162
Mercury, 17–18
Metals, 17–18, 36–37
Minimata disease, 17
Mining of the ocean floor, 172–74

National Audubon Society, 82,
    135
National Oceanic and Atmos-
    pheric Administration, 8, 22,
    37
National Wildlife Federation, 82
New Jersey, 20, 23–27, 31–34
Nishiwaki, Masaharu, 58–59, 92
Nitrogen, 14–15
Norway, 71, 144, 146, 148
Nuclear power plants, 31–32

Oilspills, 12–14, 111, 149–50, 171

Paper pulp pollution, 16–17
PCB, 19–20, 150, 162
Peary, Adm. Robert E., 140
Pelly Law, 52
Penguins, 158–61
Peru, 42, 71

Pesticides, 18–20, 110–11, 150
Philadelphia (Pa.), 35, 36
Phosphorus, 14–15
Photosynthesis, 28–29
Phytoplankton, 14–15, 28, 169
Plankton, 28–29, 169–70
Polar bears, 137–50
Pollution, nature of, 8–22
Porpoises, 55–68, 81
Pribilof Islands, 85, 87–95
Puget Sound, 16

Radioactive pollution, 21
Recycling of paper pulp effluents,
    17
Red tide, 26
Russia, see Soviet Union

Salmon, Atlantic, 45–53, 98
Sandy Hook Marine Laboratory,
    25
Sea cows, 113–24
Sea otters, 100–12
Seals, fur, 85–99
Sewage, 15–16, 20–21
Sewage sludge, 32, 34–39
Shellfish, 16, 20, 24–27
Solid wastes, 32–39
Soviet Union (Russia), 16, 21
    fishing by, 42, 43
    fur sealing of, 86–90, 93
    polar bears and, 144, 146, 148,
        149
    sea otters and, 105–7, 111
    whaling by, 71, 75, 80–82
Steller, Georg William, 115
Sweden, 16, 83

Territorial waters, 41, 42–43, 167
Thermal pollution, 21–22, 29–
    31
Tidal marshes, 28
Tuna, 44, 58, 59–68
Turtles, sea, 125–36

Whales, 56, 69–84, 141
White animals, 141–42